THE COLLECTOR'S ENCYCLOPEDIA OF

VanBriggle

ART POTTERY

AN IDENTIFICATION
& VALUE GUIDE

THE COLLECTOR'S ENCYCLOPEDIA OF

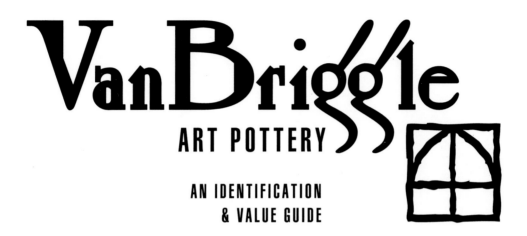

VanBriggle
ART POTTERY

AN IDENTIFICATION
& VALUE GUIDE

by
Richard Sasicki and Josie Fania

COLLECTOR BOOKS
A Division of Schroeder Publishing Co., Inc.

The current values in this book should be used only as a guide. They are not intended to set prices, which vary from one section of the country to another. Auction prices as well as dealer prices vary greatly and are affected by condition as well as demand. Neither the authors nor the publisher assumes responsibility for any losses that might be incurred as a result of consulting this guide.

Searching For A Publisher?

We are always looking for knowledgeable people considered to be experts within their fields. If you feel that there is a real need for a book on your collectible subject and have a large comprehensive collection, contact Collector Books.

COLLECTOR BOOKS
P.O. Box 3009
Paducah, Kentucky 42002-3009
w.w.w.collectorbooks.com

Copyright © 1993 by Richard Sasicki and Josie Fania

DEDICATION

To our parents,
Edward and Janina Sasicki
and
Umberto and Victoria Fania

ACKNOWLEDGMENTS

The production of this book would not have been possible without the help and assistance of various organizations and individuals. We wish to thank the following organizations and their staff for providing us with research information: Colorado Historical Society, Denver Art Museum, Local History Division of the Pikes Peak Library District, Smithsonian Institution, Tutt Library at Colorado College, and the Western History Department of the Denver Public Library. Special thanks are given to the Colorado Springs Pioneers Museum and the Van Briggle Art Pottery Company, and their staff, for granting us permission to review and photograph their collections and providing research material for this book.

We wish to extend our warmest thanks and appreciation to Darrell Schulte, Lois K. Crouch, Dr. W. Crouch, Kenneth W. Stevenson, Bertha E. Stevenson, Craig A. Stevenson, Jan Waggener McGrew, Scott Nelson, Richard Todd, Doris Todd, Chris Pederson, Harvey Richards, Wil Garcia, Chris Herndon, Fred Wills, Lois Stellwagen, Paul Gibson, and the Van Briggle Pottery collectors whose kindness, support, and generosity provided us with additional information and encouragement.

TABLE OF CONTENTS

Chapter I

History

At the base of the Rocky Mountains, amidst the splendor of Pikes Peak and the Garden of the Gods, lies the city of Colorado Springs, Colorado. It is here that Artus Van Briggle relocated in 1899, experimented with various clays found in the region, developed his pottery, and eventually established the Van Briggle Pottery Company. Artus Van Briggle, in the relatively short period of his life, accomplished what most artists only aspire to achieve. His masterful technique of blending clay and glaze into an art work, strikes a harmonious balance between design, color, and form. The influence of the Colorado environment was quite evident in his work. This was aptly stated in 1905 when the *Colorado Springs Gazette* wrote, "...the soft tones of the glaze are closely akin to the deep blues and purples of the mountains, to the brilliant turquoise of the skies, to the greens of summer, and to the wonderful rosy and tawny tones of the plains in winter. The clay is Colorado clay, and the decoration in low relief is taken largely from native wild flowers conventionalized. It expresses not only the ideas of its maker, but the spirit of the country as well."[1] The legacy Van Briggle left behind has continued and evolved through the years despite changes in the company's owners and locations, and the pottery continues to be produced today.

Artus Van Briggle, a descendant of Flemish ancestors who were skilled in the art of painting, was born in Felicity, Ohio, on March 21, 1869. It was said that Artus began to display his artistic skills at an early age by painting and drawing on metal, dishes, silk scraps, boards, and wooden bowls. At the age of 17, he left Felicity and moved to Cincinnati to develop his artistic studies. Once settled, his first income was generated by painting faces on bisque and china doll heads at the Arnold Fairyland Doll Store.

Van Briggle later became an apprentice at the Avon Pottery under the guidance of Carl Langenbeck, where he learned the process of pottery making. At this time he continued his studies at the Cincinnati Art School during the evenings and on Sunday. He later obtained employment with the Rookwood Pottery Company sometime after it was established, and through his talent and skill, became one of its leading decorators. Artus came to the attention of Maria Storer, founder of the Rookwood Pottery Company, who provided additional growth, opportunity, and encouragement. During this period he continued his painting and art studies, and worked independently on mold making, experimenting with glazes, and sculpting clay. These experiences, augmented by his natural skills, led the way to Van Briggle's accomplishments in ceramics.

As a recognized and rising craftsman, Van Briggle's talents were rewarded and nurtured by the Rookwood Company, and in 1893 the company sent him to Paris to study art. While in Paris, he studied at the Julian School under Jean Paul Laurens and Benjamin Constant. In his spare time, Artus continued to increase his exposure to the arts, becoming familiar with the Ceramic Museum of Sevres, and the ceramic collection at the Louvre. It is believed that such opportunities led him to focus on the Oriental potteries, especially the dead glazes. The formula for the Ming glaze which had been lost for centuries, would eventually be rediscovered by Van Briggle.

After a summer of study in Italy in 1894, Artus returned to Paris where he continued his art studies. During this time he met Anne Lawrence Gregory, also an art student, who he would eventually marry. Born on July 11, 1868 in Plattsburg, New York, Anne studied painting in New York under the guidance of Charles Melville Dewey from 1889-1894, and later studied in Paris for a period of three years. Anne and Artus were engaged to be married sometime in 1895. They finished their studies in Paris during the summer of 1896, and both returned to America. At this time Anne went to live with her aunt in Pennsylvania, and Artus returned to Rookwood Pottery.

Inspired by his Paris experience, Artus worked at Rookwood only several days a week and spent the remaining time pursuing his quest for the lost dead (matte) glaze of the Ming Dynasty. He established his own personal studio with a gas kiln provided by Mrs. Storer, and continued to perfect the dead glaze. In the midst of his new discovery and ever growing accomplishments, Van Briggle struggled with ill health due to tuberculosis. He had been told by a friend that the climate in Colorado Springs might be more favorable to his condition, so he left Rookwood Pottery and moved west. Other factors, however, may have also played a part in his decision to leave Rookwood. In an article written for the *Colorado Gazette Telegraph* in 1901, George Galloway suggests that Van Briggle, "...had grown to see that the Rookwood ideal was not his ideal. Indeed, he has said he always had held ideas of decoration which were at variance with those practiced at Rookwood."[2]

Artus Van Briggle arrived in Colorado Springs during the spring of 1899. After several months of recuperation, he resumed his studies and began experiments with the native clays of the region. At this time he made the acquaintance of Professor Strieby, head of the Department of Chemistry at Colorado College, who also held an interest in ceramics. Professor Strieby provided an area of his laboratory for Van Briggle to continue his work with the dead glaze, and the use of an assayer's kiln to fire the ceramic ware. At the suggestion of his doctor, Van Briggle took walks around the countryside, which gave him the opportunity to search for deposits of kaolin and feldspar, elements utilized in clay mixtures. He made such a discovery in a region known as Black Canyon, in the area of the Garden of the Gods. He also found and utilized clays from the area of Golden and other canyons west of the Garden of the Gods, and used materials imported from outside of the United States. The proper mixture of these elements resulted in a clay which would not blister or crack when fired.

Van Briggle spent the summer of 1900 at the Chico Basin Ranch outside of Colorado Springs, perfecting new designs for his glaze (Plate 1). George Galloway reported that during the time of his stay at the ranch, Van Briggle's first exhibit of the dead glaze was held at the Paris Exposition.

In a communication, Mrs. Storer related to Van Briggle that his work was the most admired within the Rookwood exhibit. Galloway also describes a letter Van Briggle received from the president of Rookwood, apparently related to the response received during this exhibit: "It asked him for his dead glaze recipe. No one knew better than Mr. Van Briggle its value, for he himself had measured the struggle by which the secret of its composition had been recovered. He was very ill; he thought he was going to die. Could he let the recipe again be lost? So in a spirit of noble generosity he did more than bequeath his secret to the president of Rookwood–he sent it to him at once. Mr. Van Briggle did not die, and since that time the people at Rookwood have been experimenting with the process; but the results they obtain are not the beautiful effects which its discoverer knows how to obtain."[3]

Anne Lawrence Gregory arrived in Colorado Springs in 1900, and took the position of art instructor at a local high school. It is believed that no later than 1900, Artus and Anne developed the logo for Van Briggle pottery, the double "A" enclosed in a square (). This trademark has remained the most consistent mark for the company, and continues to be inscribed on most Van Briggle artwork. Van Briggle established a workshop at 615-617 North Nevada Avenue in Colorado Springs (Plate 2), which was to be the first pottery plant to

Plate 1
Artus Van Briggle at The Chico Basin Ranch
(Courtesy of the Colorado Springs Pioneers Museum)

Plate 2
First Van Briggle Pottery Plant, 615-617 N. Nevada Avenue, Colorado Springs, CO
(Courtesy of the Local History Division, Pikes Peak Library District)

produce his ware. (The building no longer stands on the property at this location.) At first, the workshop contained only necessary equipment and a large down draft kiln. This kiln was eventually dismantled as it did not prove successful, and a circular up-draft kiln was constructed. During this initial period, all of the work was conducted by Van Briggle himself, Harry Bangs a thrower who had known Artus at Rookwood, and a boy who assisted them with various tasks.

During the spring of 1901, Van Briggle had accomplished combining his dead glaze with Colorado clays. He sent the fruits of his efforts to Mrs. Storer who was so impressed with the results, that she assisted Artus in starting his company. With the establishment of the plant, the evolution of the pottery company continued at a steady pace. Now that his glaze was fully adapted to the native clays and with several designs developed, Van Briggle was well on his way to introducing his work for public sale. In August of 1901, he invited several close friends to his workshop to impress their initials into some newly made ceramic ware; after the items were fired, they were given to the guests. Subsequently, on December 6, 1901, the first public display of Van Briggle pottery was held. About 300 pieces of the pottery were offered for sale, just in time for Christmas. Local residents were so impressed by the vases, that the entire display was sold at this time.

With growing acclaim and recognition both abroad and locally, the company seemed ready for further growth and expansion. On February 21, 1902, the *Denver Times* wrote "...the Van Briggle Pottery Company will soon file articles of incorporation in the county clerk's office at Colorado Springs with a capitalization of $50,000."[4] During the spring of 1902, a stock company was established as the "Van Briggle Pottery Company." The principal stockholders were General William J. Palmer, C. P. Dodge, A. Sutton, C. S. Pastorious, T. J. Fisher, William Strieby, Henry Russell Wray, C. M. MacNeill, W. S. Stratton, Mrs. Bellamy Storer, and Artus Van Briggle. With the needed working capital in hand, the company purchased a large kiln, added two small gas kilns, and increased the work force (Plates 3, 4, and 5).

Plate 4
Employees at Van Briggle Pottery, 615-617 N. Nevada Avenue, Colorado Springs, CO
(Courtesy of the Local History Division, Pikes Peak Library District)

Plate 3
Artus Van Briggle and Harry Bangs in front of kiln at Nevada Avenue plant
(Courtesy of the Colorado Springs Pioneers Museum)

Plate 5
Ambrose Schlegel at the potter's wheel
(Courtesy of the Local History Division, Pikes Peak Library District)

Artus Van Briggle and Anne Lawrence Gregory were married on June 12, 1902 on a Cheyenne Mountain mesa, which author Helen Hunt Jackson called "My Garden." The Reverend Manley Ormes presided over the ceremony and a few close friends of the couple were present. As the company continued to grow and was further enlarged, Anne, a capable and talented artisan, assisted Artus in the company operations. As Van Briggle's health continued to decline, he shared many of his skills and talents, as well as his glaze formulas with Anne. Her abilities were evidenced in the many designs she created throughout her career at the pottery.

Artus Van Briggle passed away on July 4, 1904. We can only imagine what creative and artistic accomplishments he might have conceived had he continued to live. In an article published in the *Colorado Springs Gazette* after his death, Henry Russell Wray said: "Van Briggle was a man with a message and he gave it to the world early in life—much earlier than is the privilege of most geniuses. Few men have done so much for art as did this man, and what he might have done had he lived can be judged by what he had already done when the death messenger called him."[5]

After the death of Artus, Anne Van Briggle became president of the company, which was reorganized as the "Van Briggle Company." Plans were set to build a new pottery plant in the area of Monument Valley Park in Colorado Springs. The current plant was running at capacity with a crew of sixteen or seventeen workers, and an output of 100 lbs. of clay per day. The new plant would not only expand and increase the production of ceramic ware, but would also be a fitting tribute and memorial to her husband. The land, situated on the corner of Glen Avenue and Uintah Street, was donated by General William J. Palmer, who assisted in raising funds for the project. Anne commissioned Nicholas Van den Arend, a Dutch architect, to create the building plans. With all the preparations in place, construction on the facility started in the summer of 1907. The supervision of kiln design was carried out by Frank H. Riddle, Superintendent of the pottery company, and all the decorative ornamentations for the plant, inside and out, were produced at the Nevada Avenue facility. The new structure was described by F. Riddle: "...the building is of brick laid in Flemish bond and a great many black headers used. The roof is of a dark green. To break the monotony a great many highly colored matte glaze tiles are used, ranging from turquoise to green, yellow and plum colors; also glazed terra cotta, as well as natural colors"[6] (Plates 6 and 7).

On February 16, 1908, the *Colorado Springs Gazette* reported that the company was in the process of moving into its new facility, suggesting completion of the structure at this time. Furnished with all modern

Plate 6
Van Briggle Memorial Pottery
(Photo by R. Sasicki)

Plate 7
Van Briggle Memorial Pottery
(Photo by R. Sasicki)

equipment of the day, studios and display rooms, as well as two large and two small kilns, plans were made to employ special molders and etchers, and to assemble a full working staff of 35 employees. An advertising pamphlet distributed by the Memorial Pottery listed a large number of items produced. These included plain glazed tile for mantles, hearths, floors, and bathrooms; decorated tile for inserts in mantles, exterior decoration and friezes; roof tile; semi-vitreous tile for floors and entrances; architectural terra cotta; enameled brick; perforated tile for concealing radiators; complete mantles; art pottery; garden pottery and furniture; decorative electrical fixtures; wall fountains; advertising novelties; and porcelain pieces for electrical fixtures. In addition, novelty pieces such as bookends, candlesticks, paperweights, flower frogs, salt and pepper sets, and letter holders were introduced.

The Memorial Pottery facility (Plate 8) began full operations sometime in September of 1908, and the formal opening and reception was held on December 3, 1908. Guests were greeted by all who were involved with the company, and tours were given of the plant. Pottery-

Plate 8
Van Briggle Memorial Pottery
(Courtesy of the Local History Division, Pikes Peak Library District)

throwing demonstrations were provided by employees Ambrose Schlegel, Harry Bangs, and Lyle E. Dix. The Van Briggle Company was now entering into a new era of growth and production, and most likely needed to improve its previous facility in order to increase its profits and stay competitive. (Plates 9, 10, and 11 show what appear to be promotional photographs of pottery and novelty items, and their respective numbers and prices.)

Plate 9
Van Briggle Pottery (Probably a promotional photo taken at the Memorial Pottery Plant)
(Courtesy of the Local History Division, Pikes Peak Library District)

Anne Van Briggle had been managing all aspects of the plant's operation, and continued to utilize her artistic talents to create new designs and products. During the completion of and move to the Memorial Pottery Plant, Anne Van Briggle married Etienne A. Ritter, a mining engineer, on July 14, 1908. Several years later in 1910, the company was reorganized as the "Van Briggle Pottery and Tile Company," apparently due to financial problems. In 1912 the company was leased to Edwin DeForest Curtis, at which time it seems Anne's involvement was minimal and she was no longer participating in company operations. She apparently

never returned to the pottery after this time, but instead, resumed her painting. Anne and her husband eventually moved to Denver in 1923. She died on November 15, 1929, at the age of sixty-one.

Plate 10
Van Briggle Pottery (Probably a promotional photo taken at the Memorial Pottery Plant)
(Courtesy of the Local History Division, Pikes Peak Library District)

Plate 11
Van Briggle Pottery (Probably a promotional photo taken at the Memorial Pottery Plant)
(Courtesy of the Local History Division, Pikes Peak Library District)

The company continued to undergo financial hardships after Edwin DeForest Curtis leased the facility in 1912. The pottery was sold at a sheriff's auction on July 29, 1913 to Horace Lunt and George Krause for the sum of $63,609.90. Later during the same year, the facility was resold to E. D. Curtis for the sum of $25,000. Curtis operated the pottery until 1915, at which time he sold the company to Charles B. Lansing. During his years of operation, Lansing enhanced the business, increased staff, and employed 16 salesmen to sell products on the road. On the morning of June 25, 1919, a fire destroyed the central building of the pottery plant which contained the furnaces and work rooms. Although the walls of the building remained, the interior was described as a "charred ruin."[7]

Lansing sold the company on April 19, 1920 to I. F. and J. H. Lewis who introduced plans to expand the facility. It seems these plans were never accomplished, although the Lewis brothers did keep the company in operation. Even though an interest in Van Briggle pottery existed abroad previous to this period, there seemed to be an increased effort to focus on the foreign market. This included countries in Europe, Australia, and New Zealand. It is believed that during this period the company began to mark the bottoms of its exported ware with the initials U.S.A. An increase in specialty items such as tombstones, and the manufacturing of radio sets, was also evident at this time. During 1931 the company was renamed the "Van Briggle Art Pottery Company." On May 30, 1935, Colorado Springs experienced a devastating flood; the next day, the *Colorado Springs Gazette* reported that, "...The force of the torrent down Monument creek was demonstrated by the fact that it rose over the six-foot brick wall around Van Briggle Pottery...finally crushed it in and flooded the entire pottery to a depth of four or five feet."[8] The consequence of this flood was seen in the destruction of numerous molds and records including the molds for the Toast Cup/Chalice and the Pine Cone bowl. The company eventually recovered and operations continued. Although records are incomplete, the company was apparently closed for a period during World War II, and might have experienced other brief closures during periods of financial hardship, particularly in 1910, and possibly during the depression in the early 1930's.

The Van Briggle Art Pottery Company purchased the now historic Midland Terminal Railroad roundhouse in 1953 when it was believed that the new Interstate 25 highway would be routed through the property on Uintah Street. Fortunately, however, the highway was constructed further to the west, as the demise of the Memorial Pottery would have been quite a historic and architectural loss. The roundhouse, constructed sometime between 1887 and 1888, was abandoned by the railroad in 1949. The 14 stall, crescent shape structure with large stone arches, was once used to repair the Midland engines. After remodeling and cleaning up of the facility was completed, the roundhouse became an auxiliary pottery plant in 1955. The plant was equipped with the machinery to be fully operational, and included more efficient gas-fired kilns. At first, only the high-gloss glaze pottery (Anna Van) was produced, but eventually production was expanded to include other glaze types, colors, and designs. For visitors, demonstrations of pottery throwing took place, and a showroom was filled with ceramic ware for sale.

The Memorial Pottery on Glen Avenue and Uintah Street was sold to Colorado College during the latter part of 1968, and converted to a physical plant for the college. All company operations were consolidated into one facility at the Midland Terminal Railroad

roundhouse located at the 21st Street Interchange and U.S. 24 (Midland Expressway), which continues to be the home of Van Briggle Art Pottery today (Plate 12).

Plate 12
Current Van Briggle Art Pottery Plant
(Photo by R. Sasicki)

Mr. Kenneth W. Stevenson, an employee of the company since 1958, became the principal owner of the Van Briggle Art Pottery Company in 1969. Under his guidance, the company continued to produce the traditional art pottery, and has introduced new glazes and designs. Mr. Stevenson died on November 9, 1990, and the pottery is currently run by his son Craig A. Stevenson and Mrs. Bertha Stevenson, Kenneth's wife, who is also active in the operations.

The Van Briggle Art Pottery Company is one of the oldest remaining companies still producing American Art Pottery today. Visitors are welcome to tour the facility, are provided with demonstrations of pottery throwing, and are able to view the various steps in the process of making art pottery. A small gallery displays historical items related to Van Briggle, art work by Anne Van Briggle Ritter, and pottery from the early years of production. The tour concludes in the showroom, where visitors may view and purchase lamps, vases, utilitarian ware, traditional art pottery, and specialty lines of ceramic ware currently being produced.

The Pioneers Museum, located in the Old El Paso County Courthouse in Colorado Springs, houses the largest collection of Van Briggle pottery on public display. The exhibit includes examples of art pottery produced during the early years and throughout the company's history. Not only does the museum provide an enjoyable and informative excursion for those who appreciate this fine art pottery, but it also provides one with an understanding of Colorado's history, its development, and its people. Such is a fitting environment for the works of Artus Van Briggle, who in the true pioneer spirit, carved a niche in Western history.

Chapter II

Pottery Production Process

The clays used by Van Briggle were, for the most part, Colorado clays (Plate 13). When Artus Van Briggle arrived in Colorado Springs in 1899, he searched the

Plate 13
Colorado clay samples
(Colorado Springs Pioneers Museum)

countryside for the proper clay on which to apply his newly discovered glaze. Initially, he experimented with clays obtained in various geographical areas, some of which included Golden Gate Canyon, a region about seven miles west of Golden, an area in the vicinity of Colorado City, Black Canyon in the Garden of the Gods, and in the area of Ramah, Colorado. He also used a clay from Georgia and imported some clay types from England. A clay known as petuntse, an essential ingredient in the mixtures, was obtained and shipped from Northern Georgia. An additional source of clay in the 1920's was discovered in the area of Callan, Colorado. Although Colorado clays were used during the early production years of Van Briggle pottery, today clays from Georgia and Tennessee are utilized by the company. Over the years clay formulas may have changed, and different types of clays were utilized for the various ware. This is apparent when examining the undersides of the pottery, which exhibit a variety of clay colors such as red, gray, white, beige, and a sandy tone.

George D. Galloway was provided a tour of the first Van Briggle plant on Nevada Avenue before its opening and first public display. It is fortunate that he shared his experience by writing an article for the *Colorado Springs Gazette* on August 25, 1901. He provided a detailed account of the first plant operations: "The beginning is the place where the sacks of crude clay lie at in the sun, 'weathering'....It is allowed to remain out in all weathers, at first, in the frost and sun, which contributes to the refining process. It is then taken to a blunger...and mixed

thoroughly with whatever chemicals the composition of the clay calls for to refine it. From the blunger it goes to the sifter...and thence to the clay press...when the clay comes out of the press it is in the form of a huge pancake, dried of the superfluous moisture which it had gained in the blunger, and is ready to have the bubbles and lumps kneaded out of it....After the vase is thrown, it is turned, and then set away in a damp cupboard, lined with plaster of paris until it is wanted for modeling....Of a few of these vases he has taken plaster moulds, and either by casting or pressing, makes facsimiles of the original....In casting, a liquid clay is poured into the mould and allowed to stand until enough has hardened...the balance is poured out and the mould removed. Then comes the firing. The vase is placed in a saggar, which is a large clay jar, very exactly made, and this then is placed in the kiln. Mr. Van Briggle's new kiln has a capacity for holding 200 of these saggars....For 40 hours the vase must be fired, and for 40 hours someone must watch by the kiln, at the end of which time the saggars are removed and the vases taken out....This is the biscuit bake. There still remains the glazing....The colored glaze is put on by a fine atomizer....Like a cloud at sunrise, the spray comes from the atomizer, bathing the vase in the softest, iridescent vapor....Then comes the second firing. Forty more hours of heat...and at last comes forth the Van Briggle pottery."[9] In a later publication for *Brush and Pencil*, Galloway aptly describes the finished product as, "...graceful in shape, fascinating in decoration, and lovely in finish, stands by itself without even an imitation in the world of pottery."[10] Van Briggle himself, in what must have been a labor of love, was involved in all phases of the pottery making operation. The work must have been tedious and difficult at the start, and even when newer equipment was utilized to increase efficiency, the basic process was probably the same throughout these early years.

With the completion of the Memorial Pottery in 1908, there was an expansion of production equipment. At its opening, Frank H. Riddle, superintendent of the plant, reported that, "The machinery for clay preparation consists of a complete clay-washing plant. This furnishes the casting, throwing and jigger clay, also the filtered clay for the dry press tile....Most of the pottery is cast, some few large pieces pressed; and bowls, beer mugs, plates, ashtrays, and similar shapes jiggered....Burning is done in a regular potter's up-draft kiln." [11] (Plate 14 depicts one of the molds used in casting and its accompanying vase.) The first firing, called the biscuit bake, prepared the pottery for glazing (Plates 15 and 16). One may notice three pinholes on the undersides of most early items

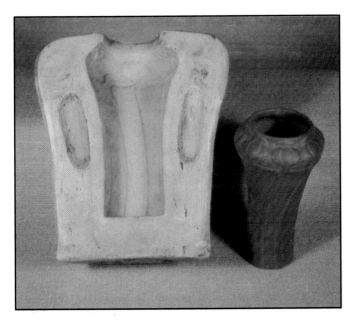

Plate 14
Mold and vase
(Colorado Springs Pioneers Museum)

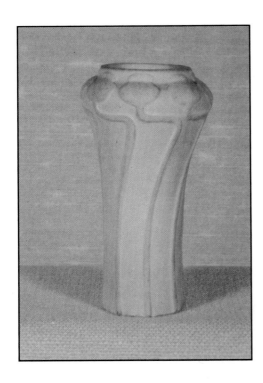

Plate 15
Fired bisque vase
(Colorado Springs Pioneers Museum)

which had an underglazing, suggesting the ware was placed on a tripod (Plate 17), elevating the pottery and ensuring a consistent finish. At times, the tips of these

Plate 16
Fired unglazed pottery
(Colorado Springs Pioneers Museum)

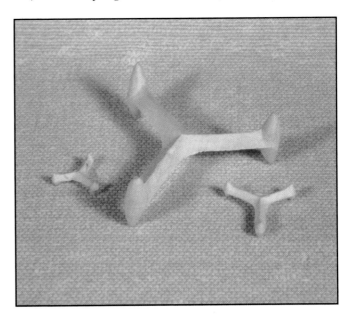

Plate 17
Pottery tripods
(Colorado Springs Pioneers Museum)

tripods would break off, leaving small white marks. Cast pottery when removed from its mold, was generally in rough condition, requiring an etching artist to finish the item by hand with the aid of etching tools. Saggars, cylindrical cases of clay in which the pottery was enclosed to protect it from open flames, were used at the Memorial Pottery during the early years.

At the Memorial Plant during the 1950's, the kiln used for the first firing (Biscuit Oven) was described as a muffle type, which routed the flame between two walls of brick. Although it is not clear when the muffle type kiln was first introduced (possibly the 1920's), it eliminated the use of saggars, as flames were no longer a threat to the pottery. Temperatures for the first firing reached 1,400 degrees Fahrenheit for approximately 24 hours. Once the items cooled, they were prepared for glazing. The second kiln (Master Oven), of a similar design as the first, was fired for approximately 36 hours, and reached a temperature of 2,500 degrees Fahrenheit. Both kilns had a capacity to hold about 2,000 pieces of pottery. The use of an extremely high heat allowed the glaze to set developing the desired color on the pottery. Today, the kilns utilize natural gas and bisque firing is done at 1,400 degrees Fahrenheit for 2 hours, and the main kiln is fired at 2,220 degrees Fahrenheit for 8 hours. The high temperatures provide the dead glaze with a texture and finish which has made Van Briggle pottery stand out among other works.

During the time he operated the plant (1912-1915), E. DeForest Curtis introduced the use of mill tailings from the gold mining process, in the pottery production. The tailings were shipped from the Portland Mine in Victor, Colorado, a region in the Cripple Creek gold mining district, to Colorado Springs, and were finely pulverized. A sufficient amount of gold concentration in the tailings was said to bring out the color and texture of the pottery. The use of mill tailings was eventually discontinued as there has been no mention of this process in subsequent years.

Much has been said about Van Briggle's glazes. The dull, velvety finish ranges from a matte, to a slightly glossy effect. Application of the glaze was done with the use of an atomizer run by compressed air. Once the first glaze color was sprayed on, another was often applied to achieve a particular effect or to highlight the vase. In 1903, Irene Sargent related that, "Beauty resident outside the contour of the piece is provided in part by the glaze; great care being taken to insure an interesting surface, texture and color; the texture varying from a substance 'fat' and velvet-like beneath the touch to something approaching a gloss, accented by crystalline or curdled effects and with color of almost infinite range and possibilities."[12]

Not only do the glaze colors of Van Briggle pottery reflect the characteristics of Colorado, but the designs utilized to grace many vases and bowls are also representative of the wildflowers and fauna of Colorado, and in general, the West. Such designs include Indian motifs, birds, dragonflies, mountain fern, the crocus, the anemone, poppy pods, aspen leaves, the columbine, and the morning glory. Craig Stevenson, a designer and sculptor at the Van Briggle Art Pottery Company today, has introduced new designs which continue in this traditional theme. These include a series of Indian busts and pottery accented with southwestern motifs, birds, and flowers.

The pottery production process today takes advantage of modern technology, however, the basic process of creating Van Briggle pottery has not changed over the years. The pottery has received numerous awards and honors throughout its early years, which has contributed to the success and recognition of the company. In 1903 and 1904, at the Paris Salon exhibit, Van Briggle received two gold, one silver, and 12 bronze medals. In 1904, at the Louisiana Purchase Exposition in St. Louis, two gold, one silver, and two bronze medals were awarded. The work received the highest award at the Boston Arts and Crafts Society in 1904, and a gold medal at the Lewis and Clark Exposition in 1907.

Chapter III

Identification and Dating

The identification and dating of Van Briggle pottery involves a basic knowledge of bottom markings, clay type, and glaze color. An understanding of bottom markings is of primary importance because the company utilized an array of these markings over the years. Items produced up to 1920 are fairly easy to date, as they usually exhibit the year or have a particular pattern of bottom markings. Those made after 1920 are more difficult to date, but with practice it is possible to narrow the age-range to a particular period. All Van Briggle pottery, aside from specialty lines, should have the logo or trademark, a double "A" ( ), signifying Artus and Anne, inscribed on the underside. A variety of other bottom markings also found will be discussed throughout this chapter.

Bottom Markings

1900. Pottery dated 1900 appears to be rare. The authors have not encountered any examples in private or museum collections. It is believed that bottom markings during 1900 included the logo, the words "Van Briggle" and a date, all of which are incised.

1901-1903. Pottery produced from 1901 through 1903 characteristically displays the logo, the words "Van Briggle" and a date, all incised on the underside (Plates

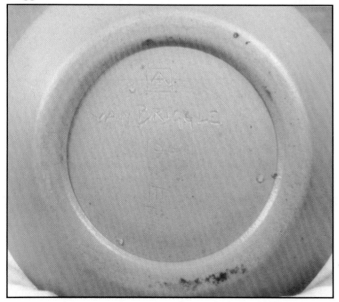

Plate 18
  Logo, VAN BRIGGLE, 1901, III (Roman numeral, clay type)

Plate 19
  Logo, VAN BRIGGLE, 7 stamped (design number), 1902, III (Roman numeral, clay type)

Plate 20
  Logo, VAN BRIGGLE, 1903, 132 stamped (design number), III (Roman numeral, clay type)

18, 19, and 20). Sometime during 1902, a die-stamped number appeared, which indicated the design number for a particular item. These numbers denote the various designs and patterns of the company's art pottery line. Design numbers were probably utilized during the latter part of 1902 as they are seen in subsequent years.

During the period of 1901-1903, incised Roman numerals are found as part of the bottom markings. Although it was previously believed that these were the marks of Artus, Anne, and Harry Bangs, these Roman numerals indicate the type of clay which was utilized. Presently, there does not appear to be evidence that

Artus or Anne ever signed a piece with their own signatures. The predominant Roman numerals during this period were I, II, and III, with III appearing more frequently during 1902 and 1903. Roman numerals written in ink are seen occasionally, indicating a particular experimental glaze (Plate 21).

Plate 22
Logo, VAN BRIGGLE, 219 stamped (design number), 1904, V (Roman numeral, clay type)

Plate 21
Logo, VAN BRIGGLE, 15 stamped (design number), 1903, III (Roman numeral, clay type), XXVII (experimental glaze Roman numeral)

Other bottom markings occurring during this period although infrequently, include incised Arabic numbers (e.g., 50, 70), which were probably used as codes relating to the manufacturing process. There have also been incised letters, separate from design numbers (e.g., DD, DC, HDC), which may denote the finisher or artist code. Some design numbers were followed by a letter (e.g., 420B, 733C), which seems to indicate a variation of the original design.

1904-1906. Pottery made during the period of 1904 through 1906 usually displayed the logo, the words "Van Briggle" and a date, all incised on the underside (Plates 22, 23, and 24). Sometime during the production years of 1906, the words "Colorado Springs" or an abbreviated form, "Colo. Springs" appeared. Design numbers continued to be die-stamped until sometime in 1906, when they began to be incised.

Roman numerals continued to appear on pottery dated 1904 and 1905, but were no longer seen during 1906. Items made during 1904 predominantly displayed the Roman numeral V, while those made during 1905 displayed a wider range (V, VV, X, VX, and XVV). Experimental glaze Roman numerals appeared during 1904, but apparently did not appear during 1905 or in subsequent years. A variety of other marks were seen in 1905 which continued on the pottery sporadically until 1912. These include artist marks or finisher codes, which

Plate 23
Logo, VAN BRIGGLE, 1905, 288 stamped (design number), ④ (finisher number)

Plate 24
Logo, VAN BRIGGLE, 482A stamped (design number), 1906

were in the form of encircled numbers or letters (e.g., ④, ⑧, ©). Small marks or scribes (e.g., ⌢, ⋎⋌, ∞, ⑥) may also indicate individual artist or finisher codes. Several items have also been discovered with initials in ink (EPW).

1907-1912. Pottery made during 1907 displays the logo, the words "Van Briggle" and "Colorado Springs" either in long or abbreviated form (Plates 25 and 26).

Plate 27
 Logo, 4 and 11 (finisher numbers), VAN BRIGGLE, CoLo. SPGS., 644 incised (design number), (late 1907-1912)

Plate 25
 Logo, 4 and 8 (finisher numbers), VAN BRIGGLE, CoLo SPRINGS, 480 incised (design number), 1907

Plate 26
 Logo, ∞ (finisher mark), 6 (finisher number), VAN BRIGGLE, COLORADO SPRINGS, 490 incised (design number), 1907

Date and design numbers were incised during this period, and either one or two finisher numbers appeared next to the logo. Occasionally, one may also discover an incised mark (e.g., ∞ , ⸕).

During the period of late 1907 through 1912, bottom markings changed somewhat (Plate 27), perhaps due to the move from the original pottery works to the

Memorial Pottery building. Characteristically, bottom markings included the logo, the words "Van Briggle" and an abbreviated form of Colorado Springs ("Colo. Spgs.") incised on the underside. Design numbers were incised directly below "Colorado Springs" and finisher numbers were located on either one, or both sides, of the logo. These numbers appear to have ranged from 2 to 18, and numbers occasionally were encircled (e.g., ⑬).

Typically, items during this period were not dated. However, at some point in 1912, some items on occasion displayed an incised date to the left of the logo (Plate 28). Similarly, items have been discovered with the dates 1909, 1910, and 1911 incised on the underside. These are found infrequently, and have been seen on

Plate 28
 Logo (obscured), 1912, VAN BRIGGLE, CoLo SPGS, 787 incised (design number)

commemorative issues and special items such as Despondency and an electroplated vase. During the latter part of 1912, the logo with a date below the logo, both incised, began to be utilized for bottom markings, similar to the markings seen in Plates 29 through 33.

1913-1921. Pottery dated 1913 through 1919 exhibits the year below the logo, and both were usually incised (Plates 29, 30, 31, 32, and 33). However,

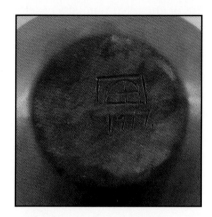

Plate 31
Logo, 1917 incised

Plate 29
Logo, 1913 incised, (partially obscured)

Plate 32
Logo, 1918 incised

Plate 30
Logo, 1914 incised

Plate 33
Logo, 1919 incised

variations in marks existed during this period. In particular, during 1915 and 1916, dates and design numbers occurred either incised or die-stamped (Plates 34, 35, 36, and 37). The use of design numbers did not seem to appear beyond the mid-teens.

Items produced around 1919 through 1920 displayed the logo and words "Van Briggle" usually in block lettering (VAN BRIGGLE), or written in script (Plates 38 and 39). A characteristic of this period is the "dirty

Plate 34
Logo, 784 stamped (design number), 5 stamped (finisher number), 1915 stamped

Plate 35
Logo, 1915 incised, 903 incised (design number)

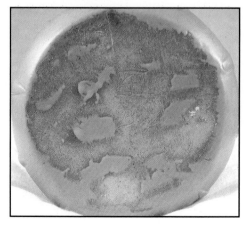

Plate 36
Logo, 1916 stamped, (design number obscured)

Plate 37
Logo, 1916 incised

Plate 38
Logo, VAN BRIGGLE (block lettering), (late teens/early 1920's)

Plate 39
Logo, VAN BRIGGLE (script, partially obscured), (dirty bottom, late teens/early 1920's)

bottom."[13] These items look as if the glaze was wiped off the undersides leaving glaze streaks or residue. Other markings found include the logo, the words "Van Briggle" and a number "9" incised beneath the words, which denotes the finisher number (Plate 40). Also, some pieces display the number "20" incised below the logo or below "Van Briggle" signifying the date (Plates 41 and 42). Signed or initialled pieces may also be found during this period (Plates 43 and 44).

Plate 43
    RFS (artist initials), Logo, 1919

Plate 40
    Logo, VAN BRIGGLE, 9 (finisher number), (late teens)

Plate 41
    Logo, 20 (date), (dirty bottom)

Plate 44
    Logo, NUNN (artist name), 1920 incised

There appears to be a transition point from clay type and/or color sometime in the early 1920's, as items with "dirty bottoms" seem to display a variety of clay colors. These include a cream or sandy color, a dark red, which has been found with early bookends, and a light gray.

1922-1929. Pottery made after 1920 is more difficult to date as items were no longer clearly marked with a production date. Therefore, dating after 1920 is usually done in terms of a range or period of production. By studying bottom markings as well as clay type and/or color, it is possible to make a fairly accurate assumption of the age-range of the piece.

In general, pottery produced during this period usually displays a sandy colored clay with a grainy appearance, or "buff bottom." Two common markings occur; both types display the logo and the words "Van Briggle" usually in block lettering. One displays the letters "U.S.A." incised below "VAN BRIGGLE" and these pieces were believed to have been produced

Plate 42
    Logo, VAN BRIGGLE, 20 (date), (dirty bottom)

between 1922 and 1926 (Plate 45). The other displays an abbreviated form of Colorado Springs ("CoLo. SPGS.") incised below "Van Briggle" and these are believed to be attributed to the late 1920's (Plates 46 and 47).

Plate 45
Logo, VAN BRIGGLE, U.S.A., (1922-1926)

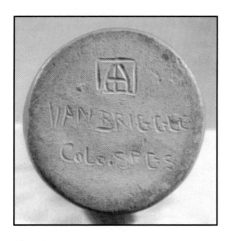

Plate 46
Logo, VAN BRIGGLE, CoLo. SPGS (block lettering), (sandy colored bottom, buff, 1920's)

Plate 47
Logo, VAN BRIGGLE, CoLo. SPGS (block lettering), (sandy colored bottom, buff, 1920's)

The "U.S.A." mark was added when the company began to export the pottery overseas. However, it is unclear whether all pieces during the production years of 1922-1926 were marked "U.S.A." or whether both U.S.A. and non-U.S.A. types were made. This would suggest that U.S.A. pieces may be attributed to the period of 1922 to 1926, and sandy colored undersides to the early, as well as the late, 1920's.

When approximating dates from this period onward, it is useful to examine clay and glaze colors as well as bottom markings. What appears to be important in dating pottery of this period is the combination of block lettering and the sandy colored underside or "sandy bottom." However, as with earlier periods, variations in bottom markings and clay color exist, which will require some estimation.

1930-1969. Sometime in 1930, the company began to use a white clay, which resulted in a white underside. The predominant markings occurring during this period are the logo, "Van Briggle" and the characteristic abbreviated form of Colorado Springs ("Colo. Spgs."). This particular pattern of markings became the standard form of marking on most items, and it continues to be used today. Exceptions occur with special lines, which are discussed in Chapter IV.

Pottery made in the early to mid-1930's continued to display block lettering, but the clay color was whiter than the sandy colored type. Also, undersides appear to be stained with glaze or contain residue from the manufacturing process (Plate 48). They are not, however, the same as the "dirty bottoms" previously discussed.

Plate 48
Logo, VAN BRIGGLE, CoLo. SPGS (block lettering), (white clay, residue bottom, early 1930's)

The use of glaze color becomes an additional factor when estimating an age-range, especially for pottery made after 1930. For example, the Mountain Craig glaze, a honey brown color usually seen with a light green overspray, was made until 1935. Unfortunately, the glaze formula was lost as the result of a flood during 1935, which also destroyed numerous records and molds. It may be that the format for marking undersides changed once the operation was reestablished, as changes in the markings on pottery appear to have coincided with events or changes which the company experienced. Another example of this may be seen during the late 1907-1908 period when the company changed locations, and when it was under new ownership during 1912 and 1915. Also, variations in bottom markings during the late teens and early 1920's paralleled the occurrence of a damaging fire in 1919, and a change in company ownership in 1920.

After the mid-1930's, around the time of the flood, there appears to be greater variation in the lettering of bottom markings. However, the basic format of the logo, "Van Briggle" and an abbreviated form of Colorado Springs, continued. Printing did not appear in block lettering, but was incised with a combination of small letters and block letters. Also, words were written in a stylized script or printed in various combinations.

Bottom markings of items made from the mid-1930's to the mid-1940's appear to be in the form of various small, capitalized, and stylized lettering. Also, undersides have a dirty appearance, and look as if some residue from the manufacturing process remained. Again, this is not to be confused with the "dirty bottom" of the late teens and early 1920's. This "residue bottom" appears to have been coated with a shellac or transparent glaze creating a yellowish tinge, and occasionally does not have a coating on the underside. Upon examining the outer perimeter of the undersides of these pieces, one can observe that a white clay was utilized (Plates 49 and 50).

Plate 50
Logo, Van Briggle, CoLo. Spgs., (residue bottom, mid-1930's to mid-1940's)

Sometime in 1946, the "Mulberry" glaze, a deep maroon color usually seen with a blue overspray, was modified to a lighter shade called "Persian Rose." During the same year, a white glaze known as "Moonglo" was also introduced. These changes may have occurred during the same time in which operations restarted after being closed for three years during World War II. By comparing the bottom markings of pottery with "residue bottoms" or the Mulberry glaze to the Persian Rose and Moonglo, one may see differences in underside coloration and style. Therefore, it appears that a change in bottom markings occurred sometime in the mid to late 1940's.

In general, pottery produced from the mid to late 1940's through 1969, have undersides of white coloration and appear cleaner when compared to previous years. They also have a clear shiny coat of shellac over the

Plate 49
Logo, Van Briggle, Colo. Spgs., 6 (finisher number) / (ink mark), (residue bottom, mid-1930's to mid-1940's)

Plate 51
Logo, Van Briggle, Colo. Spgs., 28 (finisher number), 5 (ink number), (white/clean bottom, late 1940's to late 1960's)

Plate 52
Logo, Van Briggle, Colo. Spgs., 14 (finisher number), / / (ink marks), (white/clean bottom, late 1940's to late 1960's)

Plate 55
Logo, Original, A. Schlegel (thrower's signature), (1920's)

undersides (Plates 51 and 52). The use of two-digit finisher numbers or incised initials may also be found. Finisher numbers should not be mistaken for dates, as pottery was no longer dated at this time. It is not uncommon to see artist initials accompanied by the word "Original" indicating that the item was hand thrown by that particular artist (Plate 53). Also found are items marked "Original" which display the artist's incised

Plate 53
Logo, Van Briggle, Colo. Spgs., Original, O (thrower's initial), 22 (finisher number), — (ink mark), (late 1940's to late 1960's)

Plate 54
Logo, Original, O. F. Bruce (thrower's signature), Colo. Spgs., (1920's)

signature (Plates 54 and 55); these appear to have occurred as early as the 1920's. Hand-thrown pottery has been discovered during early dated periods, but these items were not typically marked "Original." Rather, one may identify them by examining the inside of the pottery which will evidence ribbed concentric rings. Some pieces produced after the mid-1940's display the words "hand carved" incised on the underside, which denotes that the designs on the outside of the pottery were hand carved

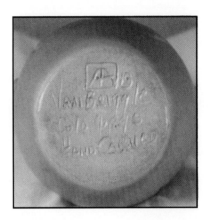

Plate 56
Logo, Van Briggle, Colo. Spgs., Hand Carved, B (finisher initial), (late 1940's to late 1960's)

(Plate 56). Additional marks found on undersides during this period include dashes or numbers, both appearing in ink. These marks were related to the manufacturing process and indicated that an item was either redone, refired, or received some other treatment during the process.

Two specialty lines were introduced during this period. In 1955, a high gloss glaze was produced at the Midland Terminal plant. Colors utilized for the high gloss glaze were Honey Gold, Jet Black, and Trout Lake Green, all usually seen with a white drip overglaze. In addition, a slate blue color was produced in the high gloss glaze. Undersides characteristically did not display the logo, but rather were incised with "Anna Van

Plate 57
Anna Van Briggle (script), Colo. Spgs., (high gloss glaze, 1955-1968)

Plate 60
© By Van Briggle, Colo. Spgs., (Gold Ore Glaze, 1956)

Briggle" alone, or in combination with the abbreviated form of Colorado Springs (Plate 57). This was done to commemorate Anne Van Briggle Ritter, and are not pieces actually signed by her as commonly believed. This marking was used until 1968 and discontinued that same year, at which time the standard marking format was utilized on this line and continues to the present day (Plate 58). Another specialty line produced for a short

period during 1956 was the pottery marked "gold ore glaze" (Plates 59 and 60). These items usually had a high gloss glaze, were red speckled, and of a light tan color. This is the glaze which utilized mill tailings found at the gold mines in Cripple Creek, Colorado. During 1968, the pottery changed locations and all operations were moved to the Midland Terminal Railroad roundhouse site, where production has continued to the present day. In this same year (1968), the Persian Rose glaze was discontinued.

1970 - PRESENT. Pottery produced from 1970 to the present displays the logo, "Van Briggle" and an abbreviated form of Colorado Springs. Occasionally, some pieces also included an abbreviation of Colorado ("Colo. Spgs. Co"). In 1970, the clay color was changed from a white to a light tan or beige color (Plates 61 and

Plate 58
Logo, Van Briggle, Colo. Spgs. Co., AO (finisher initials), (high gloss glaze, 1968-present)

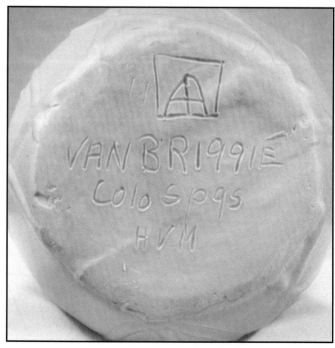

Plate 61
Logo, Van Briggle, Colo. Spgs., HVM (finisher initials), // (incised manufacturing mark), (beige clay bottom, 1970-present)

Plate 59
gold ore glaze, Colo. Spgs., (1956)

Plate 62
Logo, Van Briggle, Colo. Spgs., K (finisher
initial), (beige clay bottom, 1970-present)

62). During this period undersides usually had a shiny appearance, as they were covered with a coating of shellac. Etcher or finisher numbers no longer appear, however, individual etcher initials were used. Ink marks may be found periodically, as well as small incised Roman numerals, both marks having some relation to the manufacturing process. During 1984 and 1985, items were dated with the last two digits of the year incised in a circle (e.g. ⊛, ⊛). It appears that this type of dating was limited to only the two years of 1984 and 1985. Some new designs and art ware which were produced from the 1920's to the present, have catalog numbers assigned to them, which are listed only in the company catalogs and pamphlets. These would include specialty items such as candlesticks and novelty items (see Chapter IV).

Glaze Color

As previously mentioned, the use of glaze color in conjunction with bottom markings may assist in determining the particular period of pottery production. To a degree, and with enough experience, some seasoned Van Briggle collectors are able to date a piece within a period by examining the glaze color. This section will highlight some of the predominant glaze colors utilized during various periods, however, a detailed listing of every color and color combination would fall beyond the scope of this book. The glaze colors reviewed here are based on those which have been discovered while researching this book. It is possible, however infrequent, to uncover a glaze color or bottom marking which is not characteristic of a certain period. The reader is advised to review and examine the various glaze colors, bottom markings, and related dates in Chapter V.

The period of 1901 through 1912 by far demonstrates the greatest range of colors and variations. Upon examining these pieces, one may discover rich, deep colors in a smooth velvety finish. Pottery may be finished with one glaze color, or in combination with another color oversprayed, which skillfully accents and blends

with an etched or molded design. Also, earlier pieces may have multiple (more than 2) combinations of glaze colors, although these appear less commonly. It is difficult to say with certainty which glaze colors were predominant during this period. However, greens, blues, browns, and reds in various shades and hues appear frequently. In general, yellows, whites, and high gloss glazes appear less frequently. Some rare pieces were clad or electroplated with copper, while even rarer items were accented with sculpted bronze overlays.

During the period of late 1912 through the early 1920's, the predominant glaze colors which are found include Turquoise Blue or Ming Turquoise, Mulberry, and Mountain Craig Brown. The Turquoise Blue glaze was usually a sky blue color with a darker blue overspray. The Mulberry of earlier years (pre-1946) appears as a deep maroon color, while the Persian Rose (1946 to 1968) was a lighter shade of maroon. Usually, both glaze colors also had a dark blue overspray. The Mountain Craig Brown (pre-1935) appeared as a honey brown color with a light green overspray. A pamphlet produced by the company during this period lists available glaze colors as turquoise blue, pink, yellow, plum, violet, lavender, old rose, apple green, and grass green. Various shades of blue, green, brown, and red have also been discovered. Some pottery may be glazed in one solid color, while others may have an overspray of an additional color.

The predominant glaze colors for pottery produced during the 1920's, which includes items marked "U.S.A." (1922-1926) and/or with a sandy colored underside, appear to be Turquoise Blue, Mulberry, and Mountain Craig Brown. As with the teens period, a variety of interesting glaze colors may be found. These appear to be more commonly associated with pottery marked "U.S.A."(1922-1926). Colors other than the predominant types of this period include a deep cobalt blue, a dark brown with a light green overspray, a solid light green, and a color which has the honey brown appearance of the Mountain Craig Brown but lacks the green overspray. A variation of the Turquoise Blue, a pale shade of green with a dark blue overspray, appears frequently through the 1920's and mid-1940's. Whether this color was considered separate from Turquoise Blue is uncertain, but it was probably classified in the same category. Another interesting and less common glaze found during this period, was the high gloss glaze in yellow, orange, and light green with pink highlights.

It appears that from the 1930's through the late 1960's the predominant glaze colors were Turquoise Blue, Mulberry (up to 1946), and Persian Rose (1946 to 1968). The formula for the Mountain Craig Brown glaze was lost in the flood of 1935, therefore it did not appear after this time. The white colored glazed called "Moonglo" was introduced sometime in 1946. In 1955, the high gloss glaze colors of Honey Gold, Jet Black, and Trout Lake Green were produced, usually seen with a white drip overglaze. These were incised with "Anna Van Briggle" on the underside until 1968, when bottom markings returned to the standard format. The Jet Black continued to be produced, while the Honey Gold appeared to change to a darker brown color, and the Trout Lake Green was discontinued sometime prior to 1968. Another high gloss glaze produced for a short period in 1956 was the "Gold Ore" glaze described as a light tan hue containing red specks. Aside from the colors mentioned, variations during this period rarely appeared.

From 1970 through the present, a variety of new glazes were introduced. The Turquoise Blue or Ming Turquoise has been the company's long-standing glaze and continues to be produced to the present day. In 1979, the Moonglo glaze was altered to a whiter shade and also continues to be produced. Variations of the Moonglo include "Moonglo Mist" (1987-1988), a white glaze with blue shading, and "Iceberg" (1983-1988), which utilized a similar color format. From 1978 through 1983, a honey brown colored glaze known as "Russet" was produced. Russet should not be confused with the Mountain Craig Brown, as it is a redder shade of brown and lacks the light green overspray. A black glaze called "Midnight," was also produced from 1979 to 1983. Several high gloss glazes similar to the "Anna Van Briggle" line were also introduced during this period. These include a high gloss jade (1982-1988), a high gloss cobalt, and a high gloss gray (1985 to the present). The high gloss black from the 1950's continues to be made to the present day, while the high gloss brown was discontinued in 1989. The high gloss glazes appear both with and without the white drip overglaze. A pink glaze called "Desert Rose" was also produced in 1982 and discontinued in 1983. Two colors which were introduced in 1988 are the "Goldenrod," a rich yellow color (discontinued in 1991), and "Dusty Rose," a very light peach or sandy tone color with a light blue overspray, which is still being produced.

To conclude this chapter on the identification and dating of Van Briggle pottery, several factors must be mentioned. During the research process and in the writing of this book, it became apparent that in general, exact or detailed records relating to the production and marking of pottery were lacking. Several events may account for this. For example, the company experienced a fire in 1919 and major flood in 1935, which contributed to the loss of records. Records relating to pottery made after 1920 through the 1960's also seem to be lacking. Therefore, the information provided in this book has been assimilated from available records, archives, and printed materials from libraries and museums, as well as interviews with collectors, historians, and individuals associated with the pottery. During this process, over several thousand pieces of pottery from the periods discussed were examined. The material in this book is intended to be a guide and does not suggest that variations in markings do not exist, as it appears that individual artists and potters possessed some degree of free expression in creating their ware.

Plate 63
Logo, Van Briggle, X (mark?), (dirty bottom, late teens/1920's)

For example, the bottom markings found on a piece characteristic of the late teens and early 1920's (Plate 63), shows a Roman numeral ten ("X") incised under "Van Briggle." It was believed that the practice of incising Roman numerals ceased after 1905. Whether this mark stands for the clay type or has some other

Plate 64
Logo (beige clay/bottom, 1970-present)

meaning assigned to it, at the present time remains a mystery. Similarly, some pottery discovered only displays the incised logo (Plate 64). As previously mentioned, dates were occasionally incised during 1919, and some

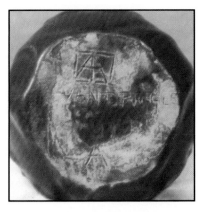

Plate 65
Logo, VAN BRIGGLE, 1919 incised,
A incised (finisher's initial)

items have been found with a finisher's initial on the underside (Plate 65). Also, pottery produced during the

Plate 66
Logo, VAN BRIGGLE, 1902, 28B incised
(design number), III (Roman numeral,
clay type)

Plate 67
Logo, Van Briggle, Colo. Spgs., 623 incised (design
number), 11 (finisher number), (plate bottom)

latter part of 1902 typically displays die-stamped numbers, but a few pieces have been found to be incised (Plate 66). Bottom markings for decorative plates (Plate 67) as well as for copperclad pieces (Plate 68) were similar to pottery vases. It appears certain that unusual and interesting pottery will continue to be discovered, adding to the present status of knowledge. One of the best ways to understand and experience Van Briggle is by examining the pottery itself. One may then begin to experience a true passion for the history and beauty of the colors, designs, and textures inherent in this art pottery.

Plate 68
Logo, VAN BRIGGLE, CoLo. SPRINGS,
648 incised (design number), 11 and 16
(finisher numbers), (copperclad bottom)

Chapter IV

Special Lines

Special lines of Van Briggle pottery have been produced throughout the history of the company and continue to be made today. Items such as figurals, lamps, decorative plates, tiles, bookends, paperweights, wall pockets, utilitarian ware, candlesticks, letter holders, trays, plaques, covered jars, ashtrays, and flower frogs, were made in various sizes, colors, and designs. A small portion of these items were also part of the art pottery line and had design numbers assigned to them. This chapter will provide a basic overview of the more unique special lines produced by the company. Corresponding bottom markings are listed under each color plate.

Figurals

Figurals may be classified as those works produced in which a figure is an integral part of the overall design. These items may be non-utilitarian decorative pieces or take the form of planters or lamps. The majority of figural pieces were not typically part of the art pottery line, however, exceptions such as the Lorelei and Despondency may be considered figurals. These items characteristically display design numbers, and they will be mentioned in this section. The reader is advised to review the color plate section (Chapter V), which includes additional photos of similar works from various periods.

Plate 69
Logo (marked on each base)
(Colorado Springs Pioneers Museum)

Plate 70
Logo, VB, CS, (1920's)
(Private Collection)

Plate 71
Logo, VB, CS, J (fin. init.), (1970-present)
(Van Briggle Art Pottery Company)

Siren of the Sea (Plates 69, 70, and 71). Depicts a mermaid reclining at the edge of a shell-shaped bowl. It has been suggested that this design was the last piece created by Anne Van Briggle Ritter for the new owners before she left the pottery.

Shell Girl (Plate 72). Depicts a woman sitting crossed legged with arms outstretched, holding a large sea shell. Designed by William Higman.

Daydreamer (Plate 73). Depicts a seated woman in a dress and cape gazing downward. Designed by Nellie Walker, and was also produced as a lamp.

Lady of the Lake (Plate 74). Depicts a woman kneeling and looking into a pool, usually seen with a flower frog depicting a turtle. Designed by William Higman, and also made as a lamp.

Plate 72
 Logo (early 1930's to mid-1940's)
 (Harvey Richards and Wil Garcia)

Plate 73
 Logo, / / (ink manufacturing mark), (early
 1930's-1950's)
 (Colorado Springs Pioneers Museum)

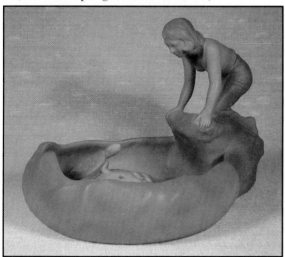

Plate 74
 Logo, VB, CS, (mid-1930's to mid-1940's)
 (Private Collection)

Water Nymph (Plate 75). Depicts a nude woman partially kneeling and holding and feeding a large bird. Designed by William Higman.

Plate 75
 Logo, VB, CS, (mid-1930's to mid-1940's)
 (Private Collection)

The company produced a different figural in 1979 similarly called "Water Nymph," which is a lamp and depicts a stylized figure standing against what appears to be a large flower stem.

Hopi Maiden (Plate 76). Depicts a Native American woman grinding corn. Designed by Gene Hopkins.

Plate 76
 Logo, L (fin. init.), (mid-1940's to late 1960's)
 (Private Collection)

Rebecca at the Well (Plate 77). Depicts a woman leaning against a tree trunk holding a water jar. Designed by Nelson Curtis, and also made as a lamp.

Anna Van (Plate 78). Depicts a woman standing next to what appears to be an oversized calla lily.

Mermaid Tray (Plate 79). Depicts a mermaid reclined and wrapped around one edge of a round tray. Designed by Craig Stevenson.

Special Lines 31

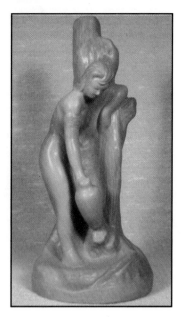

Plate 77
Logo, VB, CSC, L (fin. init.), // (incised manufacturing mark), (Lamp base, 1970's-present) (Private Collection)

Plate 78
Logo, VB, CS, Z (fin. init.), (1970's-present) (Van Briggle Art Pottery Company)

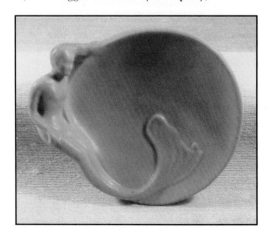

Plate 79
Logo, VB, CS, MB (fin. init.), (late 1980's-present) (Van Briggle Art Pottery Company)

Great American Indians. A series of American Indian busts which depict Sacajawea, Sitting Bull, Geronimo (Plate 80), Red Cloud, Chief Two Moons, and Chief Joseph (Plate 81). Designed by Craig Stevenson.

Plate 80
1) Logo, VB art pottery, CSC, Limited Ed., CS (fin. init.), 1981
2) Logo, VB art pottery, Limited Ed., No. 250, CS (fin. init.), 1984
3) Logo, VB art pottery, CSC, Limited Ed., CS (fin. init.), 1980
(Van Briggle Art Pottery Company)

Plate 81
1) Logo, VB art pottery, Limited Ed., CS (fin. init.), 1983
2) Logo, VB art pottery, Limited Ed., CS (fin. init.), 1979
3) Logo, VB, CSC, Limited Ed., CS (fin. init.), 1982
(Van Briggle Art Pottery Company)

The following items are part of the art pottery line, but contain an integrated figure in the overall vase design.

Chalice/Toast Cup (Plate 82). Depicts what appears to be a mermaid holding a fish. Designed by Artus Van Briggle at the Chico Basin Ranch during 1900.

Lady of the Lily (Plates 83 and 84). Depicts a woman in a somewhat reclined position against a giant calla lily. Early photos of this piece show flowers interspersed at the bottom of the vase. Designed by Artus Van Briggle.

Despondency (Plates 85, 86, 87, and 88). Depicts a human figure blended into the top of a large vase. Company pamphlets reported that this piece was purchased by the Louvre for $3,000 after it won first prize

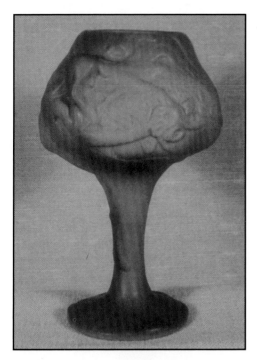

Plate 82
Logo, VB, CS, (#1, Chalice/Toast Cup, 1920's)
(Colorado Springs Pioneers Museum)

Plate 84
Logo, VB, CSC, J (fin. init.), (#4, 1970's-present)
(Van Briggle Art Pottery Company)

Plate 83
Logo, VB, CS, (#4, 1920's)
(Private Collection)

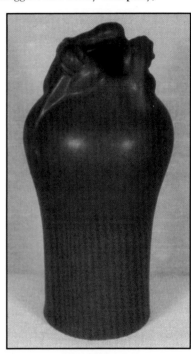

Plate 85
Logo, VB, U.S.A., (#9 [?], 1922-1926)
(Colorado Springs Pioneers Museum)

Plate 86
Logo, VB, CS, (#9{?}, 1920's)
(Private Collection)

at the Paris Salon exhibit. It has been suggested that the design number for this piece is number 9, previously believed to be number 70. This apparently was due to the discovery of the number 70 incised on the underside. However, early examples of Van Briggle pottery with other designs were found to also have an incised number 70. Thus it appears that this number may be related to

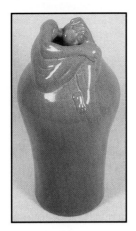

Plate 87
Logo, VB, CS, 46 (fin. #), (#9{?}, Gold Ore Glaze, 1956)
(Private Collection)

Plate 88
Close-up of Plate 85, Despondency
(Colorado Springs Pioneers Museum)

the production process. A 1901 piece with the number "70" incised, and a 1910 piece without an incised number, have both been discovered. Further clarification of this awaits the discovery of a piece with an incised or stamped "9" on the underside.

Plate 89
Logo, VB, 1902, III, (#17) (Private Collection)

Lorelei (Plates 89, 90, 91, 92, and 93). Depicts a mermaid situated around the top rim of a vase whose body wraps around the remaining portion. One of the more famous designs created by Artus Van Briggle. The origin of the Lorelei is based on the story of a siren who haunted a boulder near the shores of the Rhine River. It was said her songs were so enchanting that sailors failed to adequately steer their ships and were ultimately led to their destruction.

Plate 90
Logo, VB, 1902, (#17)
(Colorado Springs Pioneers Museum)

Plate 91
Logo, VB, CS, (#17, 1920's)
(Private Collection)

Plate 92
Logo, VB, CS, (#17, 1920's)
(Private Collection)

Two Bears Vase (Plate 94 and 95). Depicts two molded bears at the upper portion of a vase, as if they are climbing to the top. Designed by George Young.

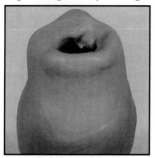

Plate 93
Close-up of Plate 91
(Private Collection)

Plate 94
Logo, VB, 1905, #244 inc., V
(Private Collection)

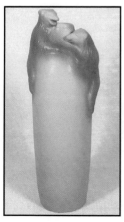

Plate 95
Logo, VB, CS, (#244, 1920's)
(Private Collection)

Bat Vase (Plate 96). Depicts three molded bats near the bottom of a tall vase.

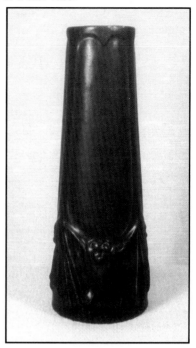

Plate 96
Logo, 1916 inc., (#875)
(Private Collection)

Lamps

The Van Briggle Company produced lamps of numerous styles and designs. A pamphlet distributed by the company sometime before 1907 advertised various lamps available for purchase. It reported that the lamps had metal shades which harmonized with their respective bases in both design and color. Items produced as part of the art pottery line were utilized as pottery bases (Plate 97). This would suggest that the production of lamps

Plate 97
Logo, VB, CS, 1907, #400 inc., 8 (fin.#)
(Private Collection)

began at the Nevada Avenue plant. Lamps produced at the Memorial plant included copperclad (Plate 98) and art pottery line vases (Plate 99). Sometime in the 1920's the company began producing shades in the colors of

Plate 100
Unmarked, teens period
(Private Collection)

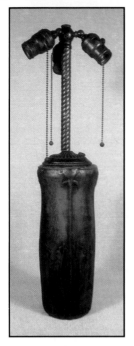

Plate 98
Logo, VB, CS, #650 inc., (1908-1912),
(copperclad)
(Private Collection)

Plate 101
Logo, VB, (teens)
(Private Collection)

Plate 99
Logo, VB, U.S.A., (#49 1922-1926)
(Van Briggle Art Pottery Company)

turquoise, rose, and green. These were constructed with native flowers and tropical butterflies pressed between two sheets of cellulose. Various small lamps (night lights) in the form of animals, leaves, and geometric forms (Plate 100), appear to have been produced starting in the teens period. It seems the use of animal shapes such as owls (Plate 101), rabbits (Plate 102), squirrels (Plate 103), and birds, were more characteristic during later years. The use of figurals integrated as lamps became popular sometime during the 1940's. These figural lamps

Plate 102
Unmarked, teens period
(Private Collection)

Plate 103
VB (1946 to late 1960's)
(Private Collection)

Plate 104
Logo (1946-1950's)
(Harvey Richards and Wil Garcia)

Plate 105
Logo (1946-1950's)
(Harvey Richards and Wil Garcia)

include the Damsel of Damascus (Plate 104), Daughter of the Flame (Plate 105), Daydreamer, Egyptian Princess, Indian Chief, Lady of the Lake, and Goddess, to name a few. The company continues to produce lamps today, utilizing şimilar type shades of natural flowers and tropical butterflies (Plates 106, 107, 108, and 109). Some of the more recent names of lamps produced include the Running Horse, Philodendron, Oriental, Anna Van, Water Nymph, Swan, Love Bird, Dogwood Pattern, Butterfly, Peacock, Flower Garden, and Grecian Urn.

Plate 106
Logo (1980's-present)
(Van Briggle Art Pottery Company)

Plate 107
Logo (1980's-present)
(Van Briggle Art Pottery Company)

Plate 108
Logo (1982-1988)
(Van Briggle Art Pottery Company)

Plate 109
Logo (1980's-present)
(Van Briggle Art Pottery Company)

Decorative Plates

The Van Briggle Company produced a variety of decorative pottery plates. Several designs were created by Artus Van Briggle as part of the art pottery line series

Plate 110
Logo, VB, 1902, III (#19)
(Colorado Springs Pioneers Museum)

Plate 111
Logo, VB, CS, #12 inc., (late 1907-1912)
(Colorado Springs Pioneers Museum)

(Plates 110, 111, and 112). Production of plates occurred at the Memorial plant and either had a design number (Plate 113), or a two digit number incised on the underside (Plates 114 and 115). Designs included birds (Plates 116 and 117), flowers (Plate 118), leaves (Plate 119), animals, spiders (Plate 120), Indian motifs (Plate 121), and other forms (Plate 122). It does not appear that plates were produced after 1912.

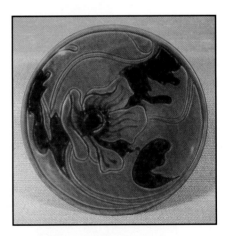

Plate 112
Logo, VB, 1903, #20 stp.
(Private Collection)

Plate 113
Logo, VB, CS, #622 inc., (late 1907-1912)
(Colorado Springs Pioneers Museum)

Plate 114
Logo, VB, CS, #11 inc., (late 1907-1912)
(Colorado Springs Pioneers Museum)

Plate 115
1) Logo, W8455 (paper label), (late 1907-1912{?})
2) Logo, VB, CS, #15 inc., (late 1907-1912)
(Van Briggle Art Pottery Company)

Plate 116
Logo, VB, 1905, #10 inc., V (Private Collection)

Plate 117
Logo, VB, CS, #10 inc., 11 (fin. #), (late 1907-1912)
(Colorado Springs Pioneers Museum)

Plate 118
Logo, VB, CS, 11 (fin. #), (obscured, paper label W7047
p12), (late 1907-1912)
(Colorado Springs Pioneers Museum)

Plate 119
Logo, VB, CS, #13 inc., 11/5 (fin. #), (late 1907-1912)
(Colorado Springs Pioneers Museum)

Plate 120
Logo, VB, CS, #623 inc., (1908-1912)
(Private Collection)

Plate 121
Logo, VB, CS, #622 inc., 11/16 (fin. #), (late 1907-1912)
(Private Collection)

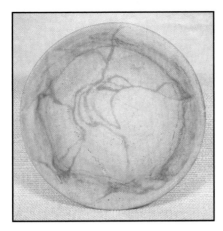

Plate 122
Logo, VB, 1903, #1?0 stp. (obscured), II
(Colorado Springs Pioneers Museum)

Plate 124
Tile mold
(Colorado Springs Pioneers Museum)

Tiles

The Van Briggle Company began the production of tiles probably sometime after the death of Artus Van Briggle in 1904. It is known that tiles used for construction of the Memorial Pottery Plant were produced at the original Nevada Avenue plant. However, production, promotion, and public sale of tiles became apparent at the Memorial pottery works. Production of tiles was done utilizing a dry-press tile machine, and waste glaze recovered from the glazing of pottery was used on the tiles. It appears that either a mold (Plate 123) or a block template (Plate 124) was used to press tiles. Tiles were advertised as either machine-pressed or hand-pressed. The machine-pressed tiles were made of a single color in a matte or satin finish. Hand-pressed tiles were decorated in several colors with relief or incised designs. The company suggested the use of tiles in kitchens, bathrooms, porches, laundry rooms, and to decorate fireplaces, mantels, and walls. The company promoted the utilization of tiles in public buildings, theatres, and store fronts. Several buildings throughout Colorado Springs can still be seen adorned with tiles produced by the Van Briggle Company.

In general, tiles were used for architectural purposes (Plates 125 through 135), however, tea tiles were also produced (Plate 136). These were made from a red clay, with the undersides carved out in order to protect

Plate 125
VBPCo st. p., 10 inc.
(Private Collection)

Plate 126
Unmarked
(Colorado Springs Pioneers Museum)

Plate 123
Tile mold, AC 16 inc. (Colorado Springs Pioneers Museum)

Plate 127
1) VBPCo stp., 242B inc.
2) VBPCo stp., 124B inc.
3) Unmarked
(Private Collection)

Plate 131
1) VBPCo stp., 13 inc., 963 inc.
2) Unmarked
3) Unmarked
(Private Collection)

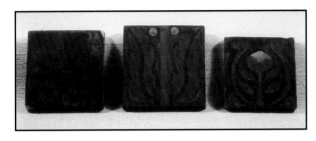

Plate 128
1) Unmarked
2) Unmarked
3) Unmarked
(Van Briggle Art Pottery Company)

Plate 132
1) WV inc.
2) VBPCo stp., 124A inc.
(Colorado Springs Pioneers Museum)

Plate 129
1) Unmarked
2) Unmarked
3) Unmarked
(Van Briggle Art Pottery Company)

Plate 133
1) 3 inc.
2) Unmarked (tea tile)
3) Unmarked
(Colorado Springs Pioneers Museum)

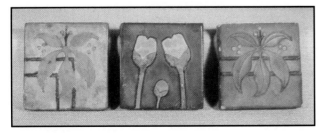

Plate 130
1) Unmarked
2) 7 inc.
3) Unmarked
(Private Collection)

Plate 134
8 inc.
(Colorado Springs Pioneers Museum)

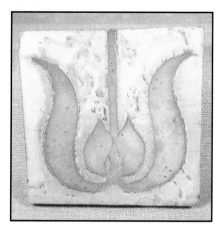

Plate 135
Unmarked
(Colorado Springs Pioneers Museum)

Plate 137
1) Architectural tile bottom
2) Tea tile bottom
(Private Collection)

Plate 136
Unmarked (tea tile)
(Private Collection)

Plate 138
Tile bottom marking, VBPCo stp.
(Private Collection)

surfaces from heat. The undersides of tea tiles are distinctly different and fairly easy to identify (Plate 137). The identification of Van Briggle architectural tiles may be difficult, as many were unmarked. When marked, some tiles displayed initials (VBPCo) stamped on the underside, which signified the "Van Briggle Pottery Company" (Plate 138). Some tiles have been discovered with incised letters and numbers which probably related to the production process (Plate 139). Tile designs include ships, trees (Plate 140), flowers, leaves, and birds (Plate 141). A series of tiles would commonly make up panels depicting scenes, flowers, and geometric forms. A company pamphlet advertising tiles listed E. DeForest Curtis as manager, indicating that tiles were produced in the early and mid-teens. An article in the *Colorado Springs Gazette* on June 25, 1919, which described the plant fire, reported that tiles had been produced in recent years, also suggesting that the company produced tiles during the late teens period. Presently, records discussing the production of tiles made after the late teens have not been discovered. Although prices of Van Briggle tiles have increased considerably, a tile depicting a forest scene with a price tag of $3.00 has been discovered (Plate 142).

Plate 139
Tile bottom marking
(Private Collection)

Plate 140
1) Unmarked
2) Unmarked
(Colorado Springs Pioneers Museum)

Plate 141
Unmarked
(Colorado Springs Pioneers Museum)

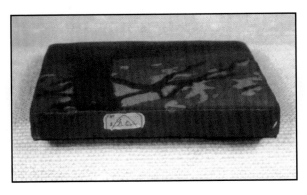

Plate 142
Unmarked
(Colorado Springs Pioneers Museum)

Novelty Items

The production of novelty items began primarily during the operation of the Memorial pottery, and they continue to be made by the company today. Works before 191,2 were produced as part of the art pottery line series. The focus in this section will be a brief review of novelty ware, the reader should refer to the color plate section (Chapter V) for additional samples of novelty items.

An interesting early work still being produced today is a vase with three Indian heads blended into its upper portion (Plates 143, 144, and 145). An early advertising

Plate 143
Logo, VB, 1915 inc.
(Private Collection)

Plate 144
Logo, VB, CS, (1920's)
(Private Collection)

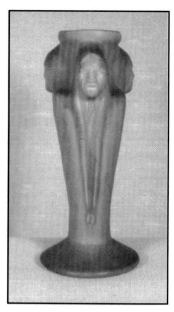

Plate 145
  Logo, VB, CS, K (fin. init.), (mid-1930's to 1950's)
  (Colorado Springs Pioneers Museum)

Plate 147
  Logo (1920's)
  (Colorado Springs Pioneers Museum)

Plate 146
  Logo (teens)
  (Colorado Springs Pioneers Museum)

introduced, probably in the 1930's. All paperweights were made of solid clay previous to the 1980's, when a hollow version was produced (bunny). Utilitarian ware such as cups, saucers, teapots, mugs, and pitchers, were also made by the company (Plates 155, 156 and 157). Some mugs and pitchers were produced as part of the art pottery line series. The Van Briggle Company also made items for businesses, clubs, and special occasions, such as the mug shown in Plate 158 (handle not shown) for the El Paso Club Annual Dinner in 1909.

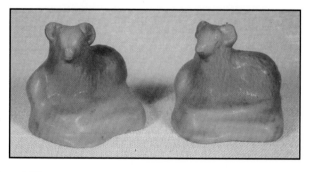

Plate 148
  Logo (1930's)
  (Harvey Richards and Wil Garcia)

card (1920's) shows this vase as a lamp, entitled "Indian Chief." During the teens period, bookends (Plates 146, 147, 148, 149, and 150) and paperweights (Plates 151, 152 and 153) were introduced. Bookends were designed in various forms such as owls, squirrels, rams, pug dogs, bears, peacocks, ships, and an Indian face (Plate 154). The production of bookends appears to have continued until sometime in the 1930's. An early paperweight (teens) in the shape of a rabbit may be distinguished by having two separately molded and shaped ears, while a rabbit produced in later years has its ears blended into one shape. An elephant paperweight was also

Plate 149
  Logo (1920's)
  (Chris Herndon)

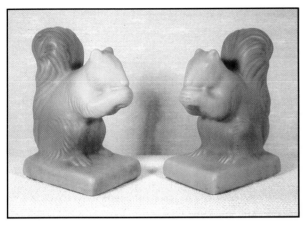

Plate 150
Logo, (squirrel bookends 1950's-1960's)
(Private Collection)

Plate 151
1) Logo, 1916 inc.
2) Logo, VB, U.S.A., (1922-1926)
(Private Collection)

Plate 152
497 inc., 275 inc. (1908 to mid-teens)
(Colorado Springs Pioneers Museum)

Plate 153
Logo, VB, CS, 1912, 18 (fin. init.)
(Colorado Springs Pioneers Museum)

Plate 154
Unmarked, (1920's)
(Private Collection)

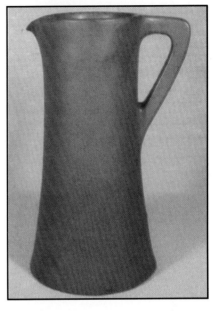

Plate 155
Logo, VB, 1906
(Colorado Springs Pioneers Museum)

Plate 156
Logo, VB, (late teens to 1920)
(Harvey Richards and Wil Garcia)

Special Lines 45

Plate 157
Logo, 1917 (all cups)
(Private Collection)

Other early novelty items produced include plaques which were made in various designs throughout the production years (Plates 159, 160 and 161). Two plaques designed by Nellie Walker were entitled "Big Buffalo" and "Little Star" (Plates 162 and 163). Also made were smaller versions of Indian plaques which were solid or hollowed out (wall pockets) and tiny pottery vases, apparently first made by Ambrose Schlegel, a master potter with the company from 1903 to 1930 (Plate 164). It was believed that initially these tiny pots were given out as gifts by the company on various occasions.

Flower frogs, in various shapes and colors, were

Plate 158
Logo, VB, 763E (Bottom)
El Paso Club Annual Dinner 1909 (stamped on side)
(Colorado Springs Pioneers Museum)

Plate 160
Logo, VAN BRIGGLE stp., 1919 stp., RW (initials?)
(Colorado Springs Pioneers Museum)

Plate 159
Logo, VB, 1902 (redesigned as #633)
(Colorado Springs Pioneers Museum)

Plate 161
Logo, VB, CS, (mid-1940's to mid-1950's)
(Colorado Springs Pioneers Museum)

Plate 162
Logo, VB, CS, (cat. #122 and 121) (early 1930's)
(Private Collection)

Plate 163
Logo, VB, CS, (cat. #122 and 121) (1978-1983)
(Private Collection)

Plate 164
1) Logo, 8/14/24 inc., Eugene Weinburger inc. (fin. sig.)
2) MK (fin. init.), 1923 inc.
(Colorado Springs Pioneers Museum)

Plate 165
1) Logo, VB, CS, CM (fin. init.), (mid-1940's to 1950's)
2) Logo, VB, CS, (1950's-1960's)
3) Logo, VB, CS, (mid-1940's to 1950's)
4) Logo, 1914
5) Logo, (late teens to 1920's), (Colorado Sunflower)
6) Unmarked, (1920's)
(Private Collection)

typically placed in bowls or figural pieces (Plate 165). Some of the more characteristic designs included turtles, ducks, three frogs, and a sunflower. Examples of the three frogs shape have been discovered with a date incised on the underside (1914). Usually only the company logo incised on the underside is seen as the bottom marking. Unusual items which have been discovered include an incense burner, in what appears to be the shape of a gnome or elf (Plate 166), a tepee (Plate 167), a kewpie doll reportedly made by E. DeForest Curtis (Plate 168), and a candleholder (Plates 169 and 170) in the shape of a bear standing next to a stump. The company also produced a letter holder depicting Zebulon Pike and William Jackson Palmer (Plate 171).

As we can see, the Van Briggle Company not only produced art pottery vases, but created a large number of novelty and specialty works as well. Again, because of the unavailability of company records, and due to the loss of material during the fire and flood, it is not unusual for collectors to discover new and interesting designs previously unknown or undocumented.

During the research process it became apparent that differences in events and dates were recorded throughout the company's history. Information on the history, production process, and novelty lines were gathered from archives, newspapers, articles, publications, and personal interviews, therefore some variance may exist.

Whether one chooses to collect pottery of specific periods, designs or glaze colors, or decides to take a more eclectic approach, Van Briggle has something to offer every collector.

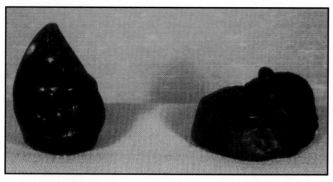

Plate 166
    1) 32185 inc., (teens)
    2) Logo, (teens)
    (Colorado Springs Pioneers Museum)

Plate 169
    Logo, (obscured, 1908 to early teens)
    (Colorado Springs Pioneers Museum)

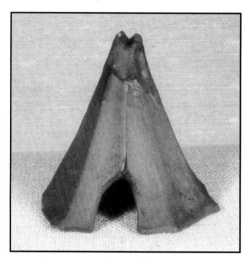

Plate 167
    Logo, 1919
    (Private Collection)

Plate 170
    Unmarked, (1908-1912)
    (Private Collection)

Plate 168
    Unmarked
    (Colorado Springs Pioneers Museum)

Plate 171
    Logo, VB, CS, // (ink, man. mark), (1960's)
    (Colorado Springs Pioneers Museum)

48 Special Lines

Chapter 5

Color Plates

This section provides a photographic review of the various Van Briggle designs and glaze colors. The comparison of designs and glaze colors throughout the years is particularly helpful in learning how to identify and date pottery produced during particular periods. Every attempt has been made to record bottom markings as accurately as possible in order to reduce the probability of error, however, some variance may exist due to obscured or illegible markings, and because information was obtained from various sources.

All color plates read in the order of top, left to right, and bottom, left to right. Each plate includes a description of corresponding bottom markings. The following is a list of abbreviations which will assist the reader in identifying Van Briggle pottery throughout this book, and in general.

List of Abbreviations for Bottom Markings

Abbreviation	Meaning
Logo	Trademark
VB	Van Briggle
CS	Colorado Springs
CSC	Colorado Springs, Colorado
# (followed by number)	Design/Pattern Number
cat.#	Catalog Number
C.S.#	Candlestick Number
stp.	Stamped
inc.	Incised
fin.#	Finisher Number
fin. init.	Finisher Initial
fin. mark	Finisher Mark
man. mark	Manufacturing Mark
man.#	Manufacturing Number
sig.	Signature

An examination of Chapter III, "Identification and Dating," should provide additional assistance in interpreting bottom markings. Information provided in parentheses is intended to serve as an additional aid to identification and dating, and does not reflect actual bottom markings. A date listed outside of parentheses signifies that the piece is actually marked with that date, while a period or range within parentheses indicates the approximate date for that respective item. Roman numerals will stand for clay type unless otherwise indicated.

Finally, when the word "obscured" occurs, it means that either all or part of the bottom marking was illegible due to glaze covering. It is important to distinguish between these bottom markings, designs, and glaze colors and tones, in order to gain a better understanding of the dating process.

Plate 172
  1) Logo, VB, 1903, #192 inc., III, V (ink, exp. glaze)
  2) Logo, (obscured, #166, teens {?})
  3) Logo, VB, CS, #548 inc., 11/12 (fin. #), (late 1907-1912)
  4) Logo, VB, CS, #320 inc., (late 1907-1912)
  5) Logo, VB, 1904, #177 stp.
  6) Obscured
  (Van Briggle Art Pottery Company)

Plate 173
  1) Obscured
  2) Logo, VB, CS, #651 inc., 11/14 (fin. #), (late 1907-1912)
  3) Logo, VB, 1904, #165 stp., V
  4) Logo, VB, CS, #601 inc., 2 (fin. #), (late 1907-1912)
  5) Logo, (obscured, #119)
  6) Logo, VB, 1905, #209 inc., V, ℇ (fin. mark)
  7) Logo, 1914, (#683)
  8) Obscured (#527 {?})
  (Van Briggle Art Pottery Company)

Plate 174
  1) Logo, VB, 1905, #239 stp.
  2) Logo, VB, 1905, #390 stp., ② (fin. #)
  (Colorado Springs Pioneers Museum)

Plate 175
  1) Logo, VB, CS, #716 inc., 16/7 (fin. #), (late 1907-1912)
  2) Obscured, (#800)
  3) Logo, 1916 inc., (#608)
  4) Logo, VB, 1905, #283 stp ., ∞ (fin. mark)
  (Colorado Springs Pioneers Museum)

Plate 176
  Logo, VB, CS, #378 inc., 18/7 (fin. #), (late 1907-1912)
  (Colorado Springs Pioneers Museum)

Plate 177
  1) Logo, VB, CS, #464 inc. 10/2 (fin. #), (late 1907-1912)
  2) Logo, 1918, (#822)
  3) Logo, VB, CS, #709 inc., 4/11 (fin. #), (late 1907-1912)
  4) Logo, 1914
  5) Logo, VB, CS, #119 inc., 18/7 (fin. #), (late 1907-1912)
  6) Logo, 1915
  (Van Briggle Art Pottery Company)

Plate 178
1) Logo, VB, 1920
2) Logo, VB, (#788, late teens-1920)
3) Logo, VB, 9 (fin. #), (#780, late teens)
(Colorado Springs Pioneers Museum)

Plate 181
1) Logo, VB, CS, (1930's-1940's)
2) Logo, VB, CS, #654 inc., 11 (fin. #), (late 1907-1912)
3) Logo, VB, CS, #757 inc., (1909-1912)
(Colorado Springs Pioneers Museum)

Plate 179
1) Logo, VB, (obscured, hand thrown)
2) Logo, VB, 1905, #278 stp., ⑤ (fin. #)
3) Logo, VB, 1903, #201 stp., III
4) Logo, VB, 1905, ⌐ (fin. mark), (hand thrown)
5) Logo, VB, 1903, #144 stp., III
6) Logo, VB, 1905, #330 stp.
(Private Collection)

Plate 182
1) Logo, VB, CS, #521 inc.,⑫/ 11 (fin. #), (late 1907-1912)
2) Logo, VB, CS, #595 inc., 4/10 (fin. #), (late 1907-1912)
3) Logo, 1914, (#671)
4) Logo, VB, CS, #382 inc., 11/2 (fin. #), (late 1907-1912)
5) Logo, VB, CS, #453 inc., ?/11 (fin. #), (late 1907-1912)
6) Logo, VB, CS, #456 inc., 4/? (fin. #), (late 1907-1912)
(Private Collection)

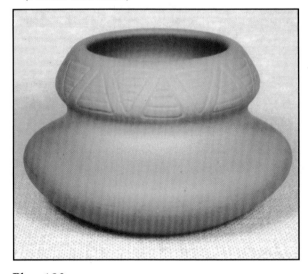

Plate 180
Logo, VB, 1901, III, (similar to #237)
(Private Collection)

Plate 183
Logo, VB, CS, #105 Stp.
(Colorado Springs Pioneers Museum)

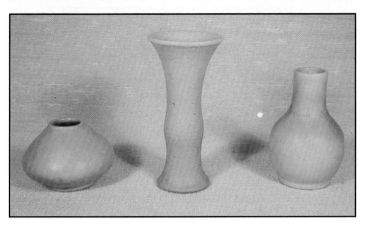

Plate 184
1) Logo, VB, 1906, #300 stp.
2) Logo, VB, 1906, #470C stp.
3) Logo, VB, 1905, #316D stp., V
(Colorado Springs Pioneers Museum)

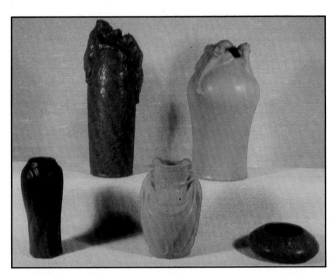

Plate 185
1) Logo, VB, CS, 1907, #244 inc., 5/8 (fin. #)
2) Logo, VB, 1910, 70 inc., (man. #), (#9 {?})
3) Logo, VB, U.S.A., (#824, 1922-1926)
4) Logo, VB, CS, 16/19 (fin. #), (#16, late 1907-1912)
5) Logo, VB, 1905, #322 stp.
(Colorado Springs Pioneers Museum)

Plate 186
1) Logo, VB, 1905, #245 stp., V
2) Logo, VB, CS, #754 stp., 11/7 (fin. #), (1908-1912)
(Colorado Springs Pioneers Museum)

52 Color Plates

Plate 187
  1) Logo, VB, CS, #821 inc., (1910-1912)
  2) Logo, VB, CS, 1906, #470 D
  3) Logo, VB, 1904, #205 stp., V
  4) Logo, VB, CS, #454 inc., (late 1907-1912)
  5) Logo, VB, CS, #750 inc., (late 1907-1912), (partial copper overlay)
(Colorado Springs Pioneers Museum)

Plate 188
  1) Logo, VB, 1902, 70 inc. (man. #), III
  2) Logo, VB, CS, #650 inc., ⑬ (fin. #), (late 1907-1912)
(Colorado Springs Pioneers Museum)

Plate 189
1) Logo, VB, 1906, #371 stp., ◯ (fin. mark)
2) Logo, 1916 inc., (#194)
3) Logo, VB, 1905, ⩔ (fin. mark)
4) Logo, 1915 stp., #645 stp., 2 stp. (fin. #)
5) Logo, VB, 1903, #41 inc., III, □C (fin. mark)
6) Logo, VB, CS, #645 inc., (late 1907-1912)
(Private Collection)

Plate 190
Logo, VB, 1905, #340 stp.
(Colorado Springs Pioneers Museum)

Plate 191
1) Logo, VB, CS, (#235, 1920's)
2) Logo, VB, 1903, #157 stp., III
3) Logo, VB, 1906, #276 stp., 3 (fin. #)
(Colorado Springs Pioneers Museum)

Plate 192
  Logo, VB, CS, #632 inc., (late 1907-1912)
  (Private Collection)

Plate 193
  1) Logo, VB, CS, #496 inc., (obscured), (late 1907-1912)
  2) Logo, VB, 1902, 9 stp., III
  3) Logo, VB, CS, #772 inc., (1909-1912)
  (Private Collection)

Plate 194
  Logo, VB, 1905, #287 stp., V
  (Private Collection)

Plate 195
1) Logo, VB CS, #644 inc., 18/15 (fin. #), (late 1907-1912)
2) Logo, VB, CS, (#279, 1920's)
3) Logo, VB, (obscured)
4) Logo, VB, 1902, III (#12)
5) Logo, VB, CS, #742 inc., (late 1907-1912)
(Colorado Springs Pioneers Museum)

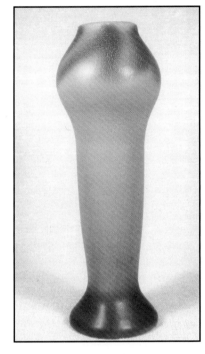

Plate 196
Logo, 1905, #348, X, (all in ink)
(Private Collection)

Plate 197
1) Logo, VB, 1906, #535 stp.
2) Logo, VB, CS, (#97, 1920's)
3) Logo, VB, CS, #397 inc., 1907-1912)
4) Logo, 1916 inc.
5) Logo, VB, CS, (#310, 1920's)
6) Logo, VB, 1905, #332 inc., X
(Colorado Springs Pioneers Museum)

Plate 198
   1) Logo, VB, 1904, #243 stp., V
   2) Logo, VB, 1906, #205 stp., ᗡ (fin. mark)
   (Private Collection)

Plate 199
   1) Logo, VB, 1910, #653 inc., 11/14 (fin. #), (late 1907-1912), (copperclad)
   2) Logo, VB, (obscured, #594)
   3) Logo, VB, CS, #617 inc., 13/11 (fin. #), (late 1907-1912), (copperclad)
   4) Logo, VB, U.S.A., (#792, 1922-1926)
   5) Logo, VB, 1903, #207 stp.
   6) Logo, CC (fin. init.), Barbecue Class 1911 stp., (on side)
   (Colorado Springs Pioneers Museum)

Plate 200
1) Logo, VB 1906, #387 stp., ③ (fin. #)
2) Logo, VB, CS, #762 inc., (late 1907-1912)
3) Logo, VB, CS, #510 inc., 2 (fin. #), (late 1907-1912)
(Colorado Springs Pioneers Museum)

Plate 201
1) Logo, VB, 1904, #187 stp., V
2) Logo, VB, 1902, #41C inc., III, ☐ (fin. mark)
3) Logo, VB, 1902, #24 stp., III
4) Logo, VB, 1905, #361 stp.
5) Logo, VB, (obscured, #631)
6) Logo, VB, 1905, #340D stp., 1/2 (fin. mark)
(Private Collection)

Plate 202
1) Logo, VB, 1906, #384 stp., ⑧ (fin. #)
2) Logo, 1918, (#798)
(Colorado Springs Pioneers Museum)

Plate 203
   1) Logo, VB, 1906, #385 stp.
   2) Logo, VB, 1904, #254 stp., V
   3) Logo, VB, #217 stp.
   (Colorado Springs Pioneers Museum)

Plate 204
   1) Logo, VB, CS, #456 inc.,(obscured, late 1907-1912)
   2) Logo, VB, 1903, #176 sttp., III
   3) Logo, 1915 stp., #787 stp.
   (Private Collection)

Plate 205
   1) Logo, VB, 1902, III, (#2)
   2) Logo, VB, 1902, #84 stp., III, ☐ (fin. mark)
   3) Logo, VB, 1905, (obscured, #295)
   4) Logo, VB, 1905, #356 stp., V
   5) Logo, VB, 1903, #41 stp.
   6) Logo, VB 1906, (obscured)
   (Colorado Springs Pioneers Museum)

Plate 206
    Logo, VB, CS, #766 inc., 18/7 (fin. #), (1909-1912)
    (Private Collection)

Plate 207
    1) Logo, VB, CS, (1935-1945)
    2) Logo, VB, CS, #709 inc., 11 (fin. #), (late 1907-1912)
    3) Logo, VB, 1903, #181 stp., III
    (Colorado Springs Pioneers Museum)

Plate 208
    1) Logo, VB, CS, #782 inc., 8 (fin. #), (1909-1912)
    2) Logo, 6 inc., 246 inc.
    (Colorado Springs Pioneers Museum)

Plate 209
  1) Logo, VB, 1905, #273 stp., 1/2 (fin. mark), X (ink mark)
  2) Logo, VB, CS, #510 inc., 5/6 (fin. #), (late 1907-1912)
  3) Logo, VB, CS, (#436, 1920's)
  (Private Collection)

Plate 210
  1) Logo, VB, CS, (#849, 1920's)
  2) Logo, 1916 inc., (#728)
  3) Logo, VB, CS, #761 inc., 16/11 (fin. #), (1908-1912)
  4) Logo, VB, (obscured)
  5) Logo, VB, CS, #685 inc., (late 1907-1912)
  6) Logo, 1915 stp., #688 stp.
  (Colorado Springs Pioneers Museum)

Plate 211
1) Logo, VB, CS, 1906, #410 inc., ⌒ (fin. mark)
2) Logo, VB, 1903, #142 stp., III
(Colorado Springs Pioneers Museum)

Plate 212
Logo, VB, CS, 1907, #501 inc., 6 (fin. #)
(Private Collection)

Plate 213
1) Logo, VB, 1906, #469 D
2) Logo, VB, CS, (#3, 1920's)
3) Logo, VB, 1905, #296 stp., VX
4) Logo, VB, 1902, #107 stp., DD (fin. init.)
5) Logo, VB, 1904, #288 stp., V
6) Logo, VB, 1905, #619 stp., 80 (man. #)
(Colorado Springs Pioneers Museum)

Plate 214
1) Obscured, (#756)
2) Logo, VB, 1903, #86 stp., III
(Private Collection)

Plate 215
1) Logo, VB, 1905, #49 stp., VV
2) Logo, VB, 1903, #61 stp., III
3) Logo, VB, (#681), (late teens-1920)
(Colorado Springs Pioneers Museum)

Plate 216
Logo, VB, CS, #648 inc., 11/16 (fin. #), (copperclad, late 1907-1912)
(Private Collection)

Plate 217
1) Logo, VB, 1902, III, (#8)
2) Logo, VB, 1903, #45 stp., III
3) Logo, VB, CS, #727 inc., (late 1907-1912)
4) Logo, 50 inc. (man. #), Aug. 25 1901 inc. (on side)
5) Logo, VB, CS, #702 inc., (late 1907-1912)
6) Logo, VB, CS, #435 inc., (late 1907-1912)
(Colorado Springs Pioneers Museum)

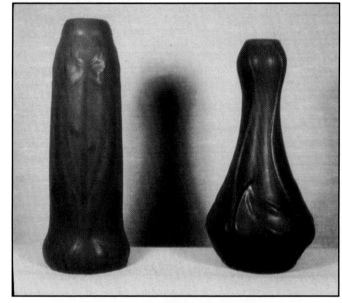

Plate 218
1) Logo, VB, CS (#133, 1920's)
2) Logo, VB, CS (#820, 1920's)
(Colorado Springs Pioneers Museum)

Plate 219
1) Logo, VB, CS , #719 inc., (late 1907-1912)
2) Logo, 1915 stp., 2 stp. (fin. #), (#613)
(Colorado Springs Pioneers Museum)

Plate 220
    1) Logo, VB, CS, #636 inc., 10/5 (fin. #), (late 1907-1912)
    2) Logo, VB, CS, #382 inc., ?/7 (fin. #), (late 1907-1912)
    3) Logo, VB, CS, (obscured)
    4) Logo, VB, 1905, #415 stp.
    5) Logo, VB, 1905, #288 stp., ④ (fin. #)
    6) Logo, VB, CS, 1907, #606 inc., 4/8 (fin. #)
    (Van Briggle Art Pottery Company)

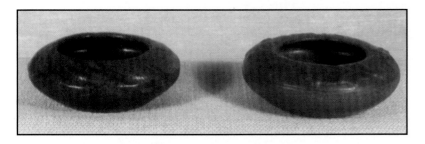

Plate 221
    1) Logo, VB, CS, #646 inc., 4/11 (fin. #), (late 1907-1912)
    2) Logo, VB, 1906, #486 stp., H (in ink)
    (Private Collection)

Plate 222
    1) Logo, VB, CS #694 inc., (late 1907-1912)
    2) Logo, VB, CS, #269 inc., (late 1907-1912)
    3) Logo, VB, CS, 1906, #553 inc.
    4) Logo, VB, CS, #698 inc., (late 1907-1912)
    5) Logo, VB, CS, 1907, #579 inc.
    6) Logo, (obscured, #645)
    (Colorado Springs Pioneers Museum)

Plate 223
    Logo, VB, (#157, late teens-1920)
    (Private Collection)

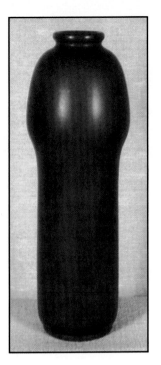

Plate 224
    Logo, VB, 1904, #277 inc., V
    (Colorado Springs Pioneers Museum)

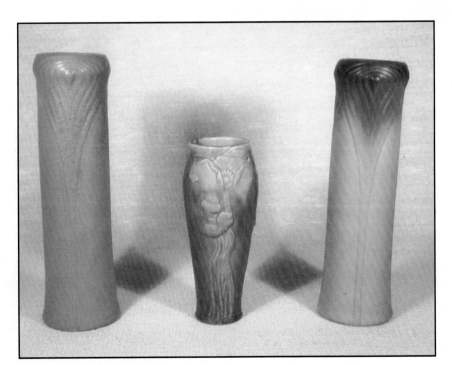

Plate 225
    1) Logo, VB, 1903, #62 C stp., III
    2) Logo, VB, 1902, III, (#2)
    3) Logo, VB, 1902, #62 C stp.
    (Private Collection)

Plate 226
    1) Logo, VB, 1905, #425 stp., 1/2 (fin. mark)
    2) Logo, 1913, (#664)
    3) Logo, VB, CS, #694 inc., (late 1907-1912)
    (Private Collection)

Plate 227
    1) Logo, VB, CS, (#890, 1920's)
    2) Logo, VB, (#808, late teens-1920)
    (Colorado Springs Pioneers Museum)

Plate 228
    1) Logo, VB, (#863, late teens-1920)
    2) Logo, VB, CS, (#216, mid-1940's to late 1960's)
    3) Logo, VB, (#822, late teens-1920)
    4) Logo, VB, (obscured, #837)
    5) Logo, VB, CS, 1906, #450 stp.
    6) Logo, 1919, (#770)
    (Colorado Springs Pioneers Museum)

Plate 229
    1) Logo, 1917, (#838)
    2) Logo, VB, 1903, (obscured)
    3) Logo, 1914, (#694)
    (Colorado Springs Pioneers Museum)

Plate 230
    1) Logo, VB, CS, #749 inc., 18/? (fin. #), (late 1907-1912)
    2) Logo, VB, 1904, #139, III
    (Private Collection)

Plate 231
1) Logo, VB, CS, #97 inc., 15/7 (fin. #), (late 1907-1912)
2) Logo, VB, CS, (#833, 1920's)
3) Obscured
4) Logo, VB, 1905, #276 C stp.
5) Logo, VB, CS, 1907, #480 inc., 4/8 (fin. mark)
6) Logo, VB, CS, #631 inc., ⑬/11 (fin. mark), (late 1907-1912)
7) Logo, VB, CS, #688 inc., 4/11 (fin. mark), (late 1907-1912)
8) Logo, 1917, (#589)
(Van Briggle Art Pottery Company)

Plate 233
1) Logo, VB, CS, #647 inc., (late 1907-1912)
2) Logo, 1916 inc., (#440)
(Colorado Springs Pioneers Museum)

Plate 232
1) Logo, VB, CS, #834 inc., 14/17 (fin. #), (1910-1912)
2) Logo, 1915 inc., #674 inc.
3) Logo, 1915, (#683)
(Private Collection)

Plate 234
  1) Logo, VB, 1903, #95 stp., II, (Paris Salon Exhibit, 1903)
  2) Logo, VB, 1903, #114, III
  3) Logo, VB, 1905, #90 stp.
  4) Logo, VB, (#670, late teens-1920)
(Colorado Springs Pioneers Museum)

Plate 235
  1) Logo, VB, CS, (#766, 1920's)
  2) Logo, VB, CS
(Colorado Springs Pioneers Museum)

Plate 236
  1) Logo, VB, 1903, #82 stp., III
  2) Logo, VB, CS, 1912, #787 inc.
(Private Collection)

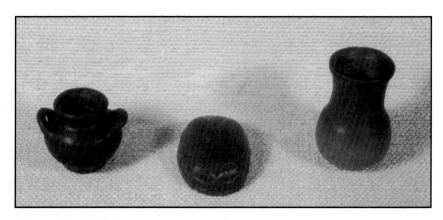

Plate 237
    1) HLB inc., AS inc., (thrower's init.), (teens)
    2) VBPCo., (late 1907-1912)
    3) HLB inc., AS inc., (thrower's sig.), (teens)
    (Colorado Springs Pioneers Museum)

Plate 238
    1) Logo, VB, 1905, #405 stp., VX, ⌢(fin. mark)
    2) Logo, VB, CS, #721 inc. (late 1907-1912)
    (Colorado Springs Pioneers Museum)

Plate 239
    1) Logo, VB, 1902, #93 stp., III
    2) Logo, VB, 1905 #324 stp.,⩗⩗ (fin. mark)
    3) Logo, VB, 1904, (#165)
    (Colorado Springs Pioneers Museum)

Plate 240
    1) Logo, VB, CS, #696 inc., (late 1907-1912)
    2) Logo, VB, 1904, #168 stp.
    3) Logo, VB, 1904, #10 stp.
    4) Logo, VB, 1903, #111 stp., III
    5) Logo, VB, (obscured, #476)
    6) Logo, VB, 1906, #247 stp., ☉ (fin. mark)
    (Colorado Springs Pioneers Museum)

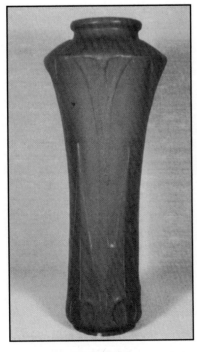

Plate 241
    Logo, VB, CS, #768 inc., (1909-1912)
    (Colorado Springs Pioneers Museum)

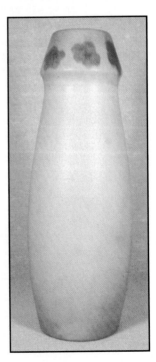

Plate 242
    Logo, 1903, #48 stp., III
    (Private Collection)

Plate 243
1) Logo, VB, 1905, #309 stp., ⌄⤬ (fin. mark)
2) Logo, VB, 1903, #143 stp., III
3) Logo, 1916 inc.
(Colorado Springs Pioneers Museum)

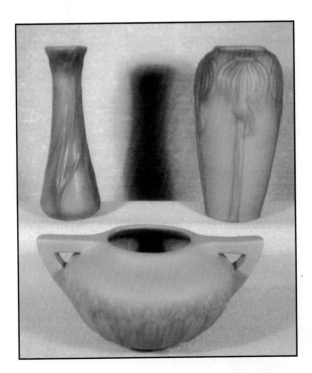

Plate 244
1) Logo, VB, CS, (#786, 1920's)
2) Logo, VB, CS, (#748, 1920's)
3) Logo, VB, CS, (#729, mid-1940's to 1950's)
(Colorado Springs Pioneers Museum)

Plate 245
1) Logo, VB, 1905, #349 C stp.
2) Logo, VB, CS, #676 inc., (late 1907-1912)
3) Logo, 1912 inc.
4) CEW inc., AS inc., (thrower's sig.), (teens)
5) Logo, VB, CS, #677 inc., (late 1907-1912)
6) Logo, VB, CS, (#684, 1920's)
(Colorado Springs Pioneers Museum)

Plate 246
1) Logo, VB, (#167, late teens-1920)
2) Logo, VB, CS, (#869, 1920's)
(Colorado Springs Pioneers Museum)

Plate 247
1) Logo, VB, (#229, late teens-1920)
2) Logo, VB, 1904, #241 stp.
(Colorado Springs Pioneers Museum)

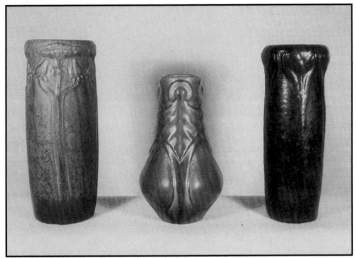

Plate 248
   1) Logo, VB, CS, (#128, 1920's)
   2) Logo, VB, (#139, late teens-1920)
   (Colorado Springs Pioneers Museum)

Plate 249
   1) Logo, VB, CS, #135 inc., (late 1907-1912)
   2) Logo, VB, 190?, (Variation #3)
   3) Logo, VB, CS, #649 inc., 11/14 (fin. #), (late 1907-1912)
   (Private Collection)

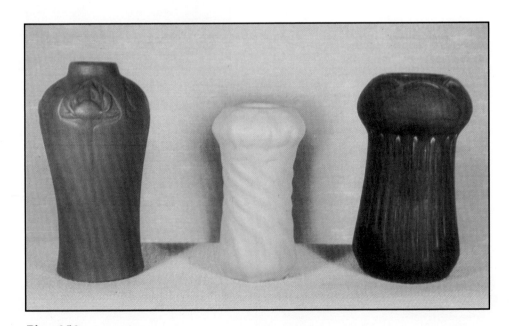

Plate 250
   1) Logo, VB, 1906, #350 inc.
   2) Logo, VB, 1903, #21 B stp., III, IX (ink, exp. glaze)
   3) Logo, VB, 1903, III, (obscured, #171)
   (Private Collection)

Plate 251
   1) Logo, VB, CS, (#591, 1920's)
   2) Logo, VB, 1915 inc., 507 inc.
   3) Logo, 1918, (#772)
   (Colorado Springs Pioneers Museum)

Plate 252
   1) Logo, VB, (#661, late teens-1920's)
   2) Logo, VB, 1905, #314 D stp., V
   3) Logo, VB, 1902, 70 inc. (man. #), 92-8 inc. (?), I
   4) Logo, 1916 inc., 1 ♀ (fin. mark)
   5) Logo, VB, #319 E stp., 3 (fin. #), (1905 [?])
   6) Logo, VB, CS, #334 inc., (late 1907-1912)
   (Colorado Springs Pioneers Museum)

Plate 253
   1) Logo, VB, 20 inc., (#310, 1920)
   2) Logo, VB, CS, #832 inc., 11 (fin. #), (1910-1912)
   3) Logo, VB, CS, (#310, 1935-1945)
   (Colorado Springs Pioneers Museum)

Plate 254
  1) Logo, 1913, #726 inc.
  2) Logo, VB, 1919, (#797)
  3) Logo, VB, 1905, #406 inc.
  4) Logo, 1915 inc., #880 inc.
  5) Logo, VB, 1905, #387 inc., VX, © (fin. mark)
  (Colorado Springs Pioneers Museum)

Plate 256
  1) Logo, VB, CS, #597 inc., (late 1907-1912)
  2) Logo, VB, 1903, #207 stp., 56 (ink)
  3) Logo, VB, 1906, #349 D stp.
  4) Logo, VB, 1905, #352 stp., VX
  (Colorado Springs Pioneers Museum)

Plate 255
  1) Logo, VB, 9 inc., (#859, late teens)
  2) Logo, VB, 1903, #187 stp., III
  (Private Collection)

Plate 257
    1) Logo, VB, 1905, ⌒ (fin. mark), (#326)
    2) Logo, (obscured, #666)
    (Private Collection)

Plate 258
    1) Logo, 1916 inc., (#861)
    2) Logo, VB, 1902, #7 inc.
    3) Logo, VB, 1903, #186 inc., III
    4) Logo, VB, CS, #651 inc., 11/14 (fin. #), (late 1907-1912)
    5) Logo, VB, 1905
    6) Logo, VB, (#654, teens)
    7) Logo, 1916 inc., (#270)
    (Van Briggle Art Pottery Company)

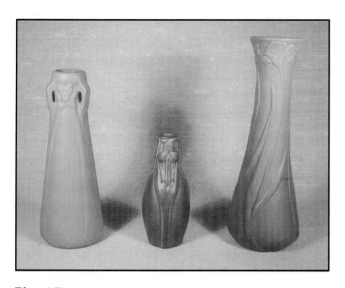

Plate 259
1) Logo, VB, 1905, #245 inc., V
2) Logo, VB, 1902, #121 stp.
3) Logo, 1914, (#786)
(Private Collection)

Plate 260
Logo, VB, (obscured), (#260)
(Private Collection)

Plate 261
Logo, VB, 1906, #482 A stp.
(Private Collection)

Plate 262
1) Logo, VB, CS, #490 inc., ① /6 (fin. #), (late 1907-1912)
2) Logo, VB, 1904, #240 stp., V
3) Logo, VB, 1906, #302 stp., ③ (fin. #)
4) Logo, VB, CS, #644 inc., 4/11 (fin. #), (late 1907-1912)
5) Logo, VB, 1905, X, (#270)
6) Logo, VB, CS, #709 inc., (late 1907-1912)
(Private Collection)

Plate 264
1) Logo, VB, CS, #362 inc., (obscured)
2) Logo, VB, CS, #693 inc., (late 1907-1912)
3) Logo, VB, CS, 1906, #104 stp.
4) Logo, VB, CS, #179 inc., (late 1907-1912)
5) Logo, VB, CS, 1906, #34 stp., 9 (fin. #)
6) Logo, VB, CS, #452 inc., (late 1907-1912)
(Colorado Springs Pioneers Museum)

Plate 263
1) Logo, 1914
2) Logo, VB, CS, #614, 11 (fin. #), (late 1907-1912)
(Private Collection)

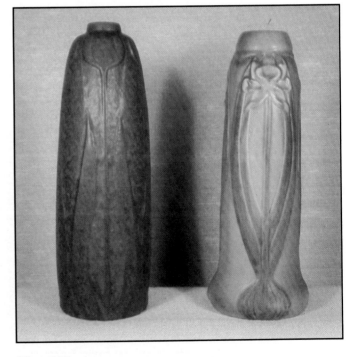

Plate 265
1) Logo, VB, CS, 719 inc., (late 1907-1912)
2) Logo, VB, 1903, #133 stp., III
(Colorado Springs Pioneers Museum)

Plate 266
  1) Logo, VB, CS, 1907, #591 inc., 4/5 (fin. #)
  2) Logo, (obscured, #40)
  3) Logo, VB, 1905, #384 stp., VX
(Colorado Springs Pioneers Museum)

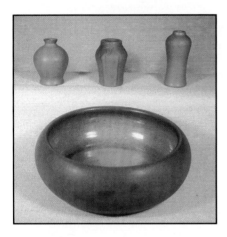

Plate 267
  1) Logo, VB, 1905, #373 inc., VX
  2) Logo, VB, 1902, #24 inc., II
  3) Logo, (obscured)
  4) Logo, VB, 1905, #420 B stp.
(Colorado Springs Pioneers Museum)

Plate 268
  1) Logo, VB, CS, #649 inc., ⑬(fin. #), (late 1907-1912)
  2) Logo, (obscured)
  3) Logo, VB, CS, (obscured, #397)
(Colorado Springs Pioneers Museum)

Plate 269
  1) Logo, VB, 1906, (#380)
  2) Logo, VB, CS, #665 inc., (late 1907-1912)
  3) Logo, VB, CS, #460 inc., (late 1907-1912)
  4) Logo, VB, 1905, #310 stp. (?)
  5) Logo, VB, 1902, III, (#26)
(Colorado Springs Pioneers Museum)

Plate 270
Logo, VB, 1904, #248 stp., □ (fin. mark)
(Private Collection)

Plate 271
1) Logo, 1916 stp., (#806)
2) Logo, 1915 stp., #734 stp., 5 (fin. #)
3) Logo, 1914
4) Logo, VB, CS, #411 inc., 4/10 (fin. #), (late 1907-1912)
5) Logo, 1915 inc., #903 inc.
6) Logo, 1916
(Private Collection)

Plate 272
Logo, VB, CS, (obscured), 11/? (fin. #), (#762), (1909-1912)
(Private Collection)

Plate 273
VB Art Pottery, CSC, 75th Anniversary, Ltd. Ed. No 6 of 500, 1974 (all inc.), (#762 redesigned)
(Private Collection)

Plate 274
1) Logo, VB, CS, #639 inc., (late 1907-1912)
2) Logo, VB, CS, #753 inc., (1908-1912)
3) Logo, VB, (obscured)
4) Logo, VB, 1902, #87 stp., DC (fin. init.)
5) Logo, VB, CS, #495 inc., 8/15 (fin. #), (late 1907-1912)
(Colorado Springs Pioneers Museum)

Plate 275
1) Logo, VB, 1905, B (fin. init.), EPW (ink)
2) Logo, (obscured)
3) Logo, 1905, #289 stp., V
(Colorado Springs Pioneers Museum)

Plate 276
1) Logo, VB, CS, #762 inc., 18/7 (fin. #), (1909-1912)
2) Logo, 1916 inc., (#762)
3) Logo, VB, (#737, late teens-1920)
(Van Briggle Art Pottery Company)

Plate 277
    1) Logo, VB, CS, #509 inc., (late 1907-1912)
    2) Logo, VB, CS, #544 inc., (late 1907-1912)
    3) Logo, (obscured)
    (Colorado Springs Pioneers Museum)

Plate 278
    1) Logo, (obscured, #595)
    2) Logo, VB, 1901, 70 inc., (man. #)
    3) Logo, B, CS, #576 inc., 11/ ⑬ (fin. #),
       (late 1907-1912)
    4) Logo
    5) Logo, VB, CS, #568 inc., (late 1907-1912)
    (Colorado Springs Pioneers Museum)

Plate 279
    1) Logo, VB, CS, 1906, #393 inc.
    2) Logo, VB, CS, #646 inc., (late 1907-1912)
    3) Logo, VB, CS, #737 inc., 16/9 (fin. #), (late 1907-1912)
    (Private Collection)

Plate 280
1) Logo, VB, CS, #626 inc., ⑬/12 (fin. #), (late 1907-1912)
2) Logo, VB, CS, #696 inc., (late 1907-1912)
(Private Collection)

Plate 281
1) Obscured
2) Logo, 1905, #385 stp., (obscured)
3) Logo, VB, 1904, #127 stp., V
4) Logo, VB, 190?, #188 stp., ⟆ (fin. mark)
5) Logo, VB, 1902, #15 stp., III, XXXI (ink, exp. glaze)
6) (Obscured), 1903
(Private Collection)

Plate 282
1) Logo, VB, 1904, #219 stp., V
2) Logo, VB, 1906, #422 stp.
(Private Collection)

Plate 283
   1) Logo, VB, CS, 1907, #549 inc., 8 (fin. #)
   2) Logo, VB, 1903, #144 stp., III
   3) Logo, Mabel (artist sig.), 1906
   4) Logo, VB, CS, #14? inc., ⑬/7 (fin. #), (late 1907-1912)
   5) Logo, VB, 1906, #343 stp.
   6) Logo, VB, 1903, #189 stp., III
   (Private Collection)

Plate 284
   1) Logo, VB, CS, #636 inc., (late 1907-1912)
   2) Logo, VB, 1902, stp., III, (#2)
   3) Logo, VB, 1905 C, #291 stp.
   (Private Collection)

Plate 285
  1) Logo, VB, CS, #763 inc., 16/18 (fin. #), (1909-1912)
  2) Logo, VB, 1902, #108 stp., III
  (Private Collection)

Plate 286
  1) Logo, VB, 1902, #28B inc., III
  2) Logo, VB, CS, #28 inc., 13 inc., 16/7 (fin. #),
     (late 1907-1912)
  (Private Collection)

Plate 287
  Logo, VB, 20 inc., (1920)
  (Private Collection)

Plate 288
  1) Logo, VB, 1905, #276A stp., V
  2) Obscured
  (Colorado Springs Pioneers Museum)

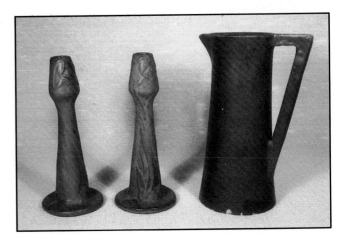

Plate 289
  1) Logo, VB, 1905, #302 stp., VX, ♡ (fin. mark)
  2) Logo, VB, (obscured, #302)
  3) Logo, 1915 inc., ⨯ (fin. mark)
  (Colorado Springs Pioneers Museum)

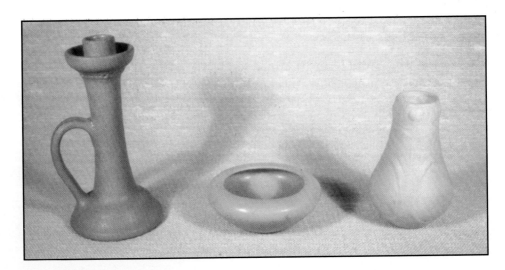

Plate 290
  1) Logo, 1915 inc.
  2) Obscured
  3) Logo, VB, CS, (#3, 1920's)
  (Colorado Springs Pioneers Museum)

Plate 291
    1) Logo, VB, 1903, #49 stp., III
    2) Logo, VB, 1903, #167 stp., III
    (Private Collection)

Plate 292
    1) Logo, VB, 1902, #7 stp., III
    2) Logo, VB, 1903, #164 stp., III, ✍ (ink, exposition mark?)
    3) Logo, VB, 1906, #379 stp., ④ (fin. #)
    4) Logo, VB, CS, #696 inc., 11/5 (fin. #), (late 1907-1912)
    5) Logo, VB, 1903, #199 stp., III XLVII (ink, exp. glaze)
    6) Logo, 1905, VV
    (Private Collection)

Plate 293
    1) Logo, VB, (obscured)
    2) Logo, VB, CS, 1907, #402 inc., 8/6 (fin. #)
    3) Logo, 1915 inc., #649 inc.
    (Private Collection)

Plate 294
1) Logo, VB, CS, 1907, #535 inc.
2) Logo, VB, 1906, #296 stp., 8 (fin. #)
3) Logo, VB, 1903, #132 stp., III
4) Logo, VB, CS, #795 inc., 18/7 (fin. #),
   (1909-1912)
5) Logo, VB, CS, 1906, #540 inc., ⬚ (fin. mark)
(Private Collection)

Plate 296
1) Logo, VB, CS, #721 inc., 15/7 (fin. #), (late 1907-1912)
2) Logo, VB, CS, (#49, 1920's)
(Private Collection)

Plate 295
1) Logo, VB, 1905, #335 stp., D (fin. init.)
2) Logo, VB, CS, (#833, 1920's)
3) Logo, VB, 1903, #187 stp., III
4) Logo, (obscured)
5) Logo, VB, CS, #635 inc., 11/5 (fin. #),
   (late 1907-1912)
6) Logo, VB, 1905, #247 stp., X
(Private Collection)

Plate 297
1) Logo, VB, CS, #696 inc., 11/7 (fin. #),
   (late 1907-1912)
2) Logo, VB, 20 inc., (1920)
3) Logo, VB, CS, #430 inc., 4/10 (fin. #),
   (late 1907-1912)
4) Logo, VB, CS, (#747, mid-1930's to mid-1940's)
5) Logo, 1915 inc., (hand thrown)
6) Logo, VB, (#695, late teens - 1920)
(Private Collection)

Plate 298
1) Logo, VB, 20 inc., (#645, 1920)
2) Logo, 1914, (#840)
3) Logo, 1916 stp., (#688)
4) Logo, VB, CS, 1912, #733 C inc., 11 (fin. #)
5) Logo, VB, (late teens-1920)
(Private Collection)

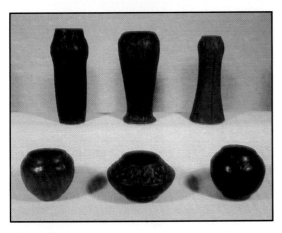

Plate 299
1) Logo, VB, (obscured, #25)
2) Logo, VB, U.S.A., (#503, 1922-1926)
3) Logo, VB, CS, #381 inc., (late 1907-1912)
4) Logo, VB, (#695, late teens-1920)
5) Logo, 1919, RFS inc. (fin. init.), (#735)
6) Logo, VB, (#847, late teens-1920)
(Private Collection)

Plate 300
1) Unmarked (1950's)
2) Logo, VB, CS, (obscured, #544)
(Private Collection)

Plate 301
1) Logo, VB, (#863, late teens-1920)
2) Logo, VB, (#49, late teens-1920)
3) Logo, VB, CS, (#398, 1920's)
4) Logo, VB, CS, (#688, mid-1930's to mid-1940's)
5) Logo, VB, (#858, late teens-1920)
6) Logo, VB, CS, (#678, 1920's)
(Chris Herndon)

Plate 302
1) Logo, 1915 stp., #902 stp.
2) Logo, 1915 inc., (obscured)
3) Logo, 1915 stp., #902 stp.
(Colorado Springs Pioneers Museum)

Plate 303
1) Logo, VB, X(?), (#754, late teens-1920)
2) Logo, VB, 9 (fin. #), (#654, late teens)
3) Logo, 1914
(Private Collection)

Plate 304
  Logo, VB, CS, (#754, 1920's)
  (Private Collection)

Plate 305
  1) Logo, 1918, (#852)
  2) Logo, 1916 inc., (#45)
  3) Logo, VB, 9 (fin. #), (#859, late teens)
  4) Logo, VB, 20, (#838, 1920)
  5) Logo, VB, 9 (fin. #), (#849, late teens)
  6) Logo, VB, 9 (fin. #), (#838, late teens)
  (Private Collection)

Plate 306
  1) Logo, VB, U.S.A., (#589, 1922-1926)
  2) Logo, VB, (#735, late teens-1920)
  3) Logo, VB, (#766, late teens-1920)
  (Private Collection)

Plate 307
1) Logo, 1917
2) Logo, 1916 inc., (#857)
3) Logo, 1917
4) Logo, 1918, (#683)
5) Logo, 1916 inc., (#654)
6) Logo, VB, CS, #194 inc., 11/8 (fin. #), (late 1907-1912)
(Private Collection)

Plate 308
Logo, 1916 inc.
(Private Collection)

Plate 309
1) Logo, VB, CS, (#843, mid-1930's to mid-1940's)
2) Logo, VB, CS, (#780, 1920's)
3) Logo, VB, U.S.A., (#860, 1922-1926)
4) Logo, VB, U.S.A., (#678, 1922-1926)
5) Logo, VB, CS, 33 (fin. #),(cat. #647, mid-1930's to mid-1940's)
6) Logo, VB, U.S.A., (1922-1926)
(Private Collection)

Plate 310
    1) Logo, VB, CS, (#738, 1920's)
    2) Logo, VB, (#824, late teens-1920)
    3) Logo, VB, CS, (#860, 1920's)
    4) Logo, VB, (#688, late teens-1920)
    5) Logo, VB, CS, (cat. #18, 1920's)
    6) Logo, VB, (#733, late teens-1920)
    (Private Collection)

Plate 311
    1) Logo, VB, U.S.A., (#748, 1922-1926)
    2) Logo, VB, (#142, late teens-1920)
    (Private Collection)

Plate 312
  1) Logo, VB, (#903, late teens-1920)
  2) Logo, VB, (#510, late teens-1920)
  3) Logo, VB, (#903 D, late teens-1920)
  4) Logo, VB, (#776, late teens-1920)
  (Private Collection)

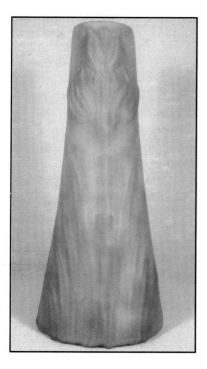

Plate 313
  Logo, VB, U.S.A., (#157, 1922-1926)
  (Private Collection)

Plate 314
  1) Logo, VB, 20, (903 D, 1920)
  2) Logo, 1914, (#608)
  3) Unmarked, (flower frog, teens)
  4) Logo, (flower frog, teens)
  (Private Collection)

Plate 315
   1) Logo, VB, 20 inc., (#738, 1920)
   2) Logo, VB, (#167, late teens-1920)
   3) Logo, VB, CS, (1920's)
   (Private Collection)

Plate 316
   1) Logo, 1916, (#903)
   2) Logo, VB, (#903 E, late teens-1920)
   (Harvey Richards and Wil Garcia)

Plate 317
   1) Logo, VB, CS, (#216, 1920's)
   2) Logo, VB, U.S.A., (#661, 1922-1926)
   3) Logo, VB, CS, (#522, 1920's)
   4) Logo, VB, 9 inc., (#781 late teens)
   (Private Collection)

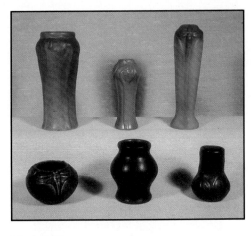

Plate 318
   1) Logo, VB, CS, (#738, 1920's)
   2) Logo, 1914, (#671)
   3) Logo, VB, CS, (#398, 1920's)
   4) Logo, 1915 inc., (#837)
   5) Logo, VB, 20, (hand thrown, 1920)
   6) Logo, VB, CS, (#645, 1920's)
   (Private Collection)

Plate 319
   1) Logo, VB, 20 inc., (#903D, 1920)
   2) Logo, VB, U.S.A., (#863, 1922-1926)
   3) Logo, VB, U.S.A., (#858, 1922-1926)
   (Private Collection)

Plate 320
1) Logo, 1920, NUNN (fin. name), (#645)
2) Logo, Original, A. Schlegel (thrower's sig.), (1920's)
3) Logo, VB, 20, (#833, 1920)
4) Logo, Original, CS, O.F. Bruce (thrower's sig.), (1920's)
5) Logo, 1918, (#688)
6) Logo, 1914
(Private Collection)

Plate 321
1) Logo, VB, U.S.A., (#681, 1922-1926)
2) Logo, VB, CS, (#747, 1920's)
3) Logo, VB, CS, (#824, 1920's)
(Private Collection)

Plate 322
1) Logo, VB, (#792, late teens-1920)
2) Logo, VB, U.S.A. (#852, 1922-1926)
3) Logo, VB, (#824, late teens-1920)
(Private Collection)

Plate 323
1) Logo, VB, CS, (pair, C.S. #4, 1920's)
2) Logo, VB, U.S.A., (#841, 1922-1926)
3) Logo, VB, CS, (#794, mid-1930's to mid-1940's)
4) Logo, VB, U.S.A., (#859, 1922-1926)
5) Logo, VB, U.S.A., (#833, 1922-1926)
6) Logo, VB, CS, (#21, mid-1930's to mid-1940's)
(Private Collection)

Plate 324
1) Logo, VB, CS, (#851, 1920's)
2) Logo, VB, CS, (cat. #505, mid-1940's to late 1960's)
3) Logo, VB, CS, 77 (fin. #), (#833, mid-1930's to mid-1940's)
4) Logo, VB, CS, (#833, 1920's)
5) Logo, VB, CS, (#747, mid-1940's to 1950's)
6) Logo, VB, CS, (1920's)
(Private Collection)

Plate 325
    1) Logo, VB, CS, (1950's-1960's)
    2) Logo, VB, CS, (1950's-1960's)
    3) Logo, VB, CS, (1920's)
    (Private Collection)

Plate 326
    1) Logo, VB, CS, 5 (fin. #), (mid-1940's to 1960's)
    2) Logo, VB, U.S.A., (#852, 1922-1926)
    3) Logo, VB, CS, (#722, 1920's)
    (Private Collection)

Plate 327
    1) Logo, (pair, ram bookends, teens)
    2) Logo, (pair, peacock bookends, 1920's)
    (Private Collection)

Plate 328
1) Logo, 9 (fin. #), (pair, owl bookends, late teens)
2) VB, (squirrel bookend, mid-1930's to mid-1940's)
(Private Collection)

Plate 329
1) Logo, VB, U.S.A., (pair, owl bookends, 1922-1926)
2) Logo, (pair, peacock bookends, teens)
3) Logo, VB, CS, #28B inc., 4/11 (fin. #), (late 1907-1912)
4) Logo, 1915 inc.
5) Logo, 1914
(Van Briggle Art Pottery Company)

Plate 330
1) Logo, (1920's)
2) Logo, (mid-1940's to 1950's)
3) Unmarked, (1920's)
4) Logo, (mid-1940's to 1950's)
(Private Collection)

Plate 331
    Unmarked, (Siren of the Sea flower frog, 1920's)
    (Private Collection)

Plate 332
    1) Logo, (teens period)
    2) Unmarked, (tile clay, teens period)
    3) Logo, (1920's)
    4) Logo, (1920's)
    5) Unmarked, (tile clay, teens period)
    (Private Collection)

Plate 333
    1) Logo, VB, U.S.A., (#698, 1922-1926)
    2) Logo, (1920's)
    3) Logo, 1912, (#194)
    4) Logo, VB, CSC, Original, (1979-1983)
    5) Logo, VB, Original, JR (thrower's init.), (1982-1983)
    6) Logo, VB, CS, 1912 (cup and saucer)
    7) Logo, (1920's)
    (Private Collection)

Plate 334
  1) Logo, (early 1980's)
  2) Logo, VB, CS, (1920's)
  3) Logo, (1920's)
  (Private Collection)

Plate 335
  1) Logo, (pair, candleholders, mid-1940's to 1950's)
  2) Logo, VB, CS, (pair, candleholders, mid-1940's to 1950's)
  3) Logo, (mid-1930's to mid-1940's)
  4) Logo, VB, CS, 22 (fin. #), (1950's-1960's)
  5) Logo, VB, CS, (1920's)
  (Chris Herndon)

Plate 336
  1) Logo, 1918
  2) Logo (late teens-1920)
  3) Logo (mid-1930's to mid-1940's)
  (Colorado Springs Pioneers Museum)

Plate 337
1) Logo, VB, CS, (early 1930's)
2) Logo, VB, CSC, MP (fin. init.), IV
(inc. man. mark), (1970's)
(Colorado Springs Pioneers Museum)

Plate 338
1) Logo, VB, CS, (mid-1940's to 1950's)
2) Logo, VB, CS, 12 (fin. #), F (fin. init.),
(mid-1940's to 1950's)
3) Logo, VB, CS, VI (ink, man. mark)
(Colorado Springs Pioneers Museum)

Plate 339
1) Logo, VB, U.S.A., (#774, 1922-1926)
2) Logo, VB, U.S.A., (#774, 1922-1926)
(Private Collection)

Plate 340
1) Logo, VB, U.S.A., (#774, 1922-1926)
2) Logo, VB, CS, (#774, 1920's)
(Private Collection)

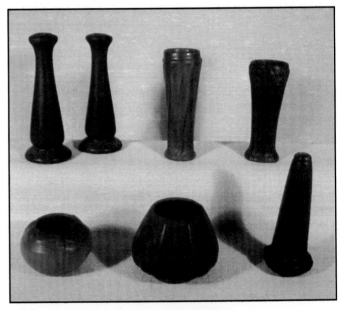

Plate 341
1) Logo, VB, CS, (pair, C.S. #4, 1920's)
2) Logo, VB, CS, (#863, early 1930's)
3) Logo, VB, U.S.A., (#822, 1922-1926)
4) Logo, VB, (#837, late teens to 1920)
5) Logo, VB, CS, (#747, 1920's)
6) Logo, VB, (late teens to 1920)
(Private Collection)

Plate 342
1) Logo, VB, CS, ≡ (inc. man. mark)
   (single, C.S. #7, 1920's)
2) Logo, VB, CS, (single, C. S. #7, 1920's)
3) Logo, VB, CS, (#859, early 1930's)
4) Logo, VB, CS, (early 1930's)
5) Logo, VB, U.S.A., (#841, 1922-1926)
6) Logo, VB, CS, (#688, early 1930's)
(Harvey Richards and Wil Garcia)

Plate 344
1) Logo, VB, U.S.A., (#822, 1922-1926)
2) Logo, VB, CS, (small version of #808, early 1930's)
3) Logo, VB, U.S.A., (#792, 1922-1926)
4) Logo, VB, CS, (#841, 1920's)
5) Logo, VB, CS, (1920's)
6) Logo, VB, U.S.A., (#841, 1922-1926)
(Private Collection)

Plate 343
1) Logo, VB, CS, (single, C. S. #7, 1920's)
2) Logo, VB, CS, (#503, mid-1930's to mid-1940's)
3) Logo, VB, CS, (mid-1930's to mid-1940's)
4) Logo, VB, (small version of #858, late teens to 1920)
5) Logo, VB, 1914 (#3)
(Private Collection)

Plate 345
1) Logo, VB, CS, (early 1930's)
2) Logo, VB, CS, (#21, early 1930's)
3) Logo, VB, CS, (#3, early 1930's)
4) Logo, VB, U.S.A., (#684, 1922-1926)
5) Logo, VB, CS, (#684, 1920's)
(Private Collection)

Plate 346
1) Logo, VB, CS, (early 1930's)
2) Logo, VB, CS, (mid-1940's to 1960's)
3) Logo, VB, CS, (cat. #262, 1950's-1970's)
4) Logo, VB, CS, (#858, 1920's)
5) Logo, (1960's-1970's)
6) Logo, VB, CS, 32 (fin. #), ||| (ink, man. mark),
   (cat. #734), (mid-1940's to 1960's)
(Private Collection)

Plate 348
1) Logo, VB, CS, Hand Carved, B (fin. init.), (1960's)
2) Logo, (1950's-1960's)
3) Logo, VB, CS, Original, N (thrower's init.),
   ||| (ink, man. mark), (1950's-1960's)
4) Logo, VB, CS, EZ (fin. init.), (1979-1983)
5) Logo, VB, CS, (1979-1983)
6) Logo, VB, CS, (mid-1940's to 1950's)
7) Logo, VB, CS, (sugar, mid-1930's to mid-1940's)
8) Logo, VB, CS, (creamer, mid-1930's to mid-1940's)
(Harvey Richards and Wil Garcia)

Plate 347
1) Logo, VB, CS, (#681, 1920's)
2) Logo, (#522, mid-1940's to 1950's)
3) Logo, VB, CS, (#834, 1920's)
4) Logo, VB, CS, (#684, mid-1940's to 1950's)
5) Logo, VB, U.S.A., (#681, 1922-1926)
6) Logo, VB, CS, (#834, 1920's)
(Harvey Richards and Wil Garcia)

Plate 349
1) Logo, VB, CS, (cat. #71, 1950's-1960's)
2) Logo, VB, CS, (cat. #160 B, mid-1940's to 1960's)
3) Logo, (cat. #322, 1978-1983)
4) Logo, VB, CS, 37 (fin. #), (cat. #19, mid-1940's to 1950's)
5) Logo, VB, CS, (cat. #54, mid-1940's to 1950's)
(Harvey Richards and Wil Garcia)

Plate 350
1) Logo, VB, CS, Original, 47 (fin. #), (1950's-1960's)
2) Logo, VB, CS, (mid-1940's to 1960's)
3) Logo, VB, CS, (mid-1940's to 1950's)
4) Logo, VB, CS, (mid-1940's to 1950's)
5) Logo, VB, CS, Original, (pair, candleholders, mid-1940's to 1950's)
(Private Collection)

Plate 351
Logo, VB, CS, (late 1940's)
(Colorado Springs Pioneers Museum)

Plate 352
1) Logo, VB, CS, (mid-1930's to mid-1940's)
2) Logo, VB, CS, EO (fin. init.), (cat. #3261, 1978-1983)
3) Logo, VB, CS, 8 (fLn. #), (1950's-1960's)
4) Logo, VB, CS, V (inc., man. mark), PG (thrower's init.), (1970's)
5) Logo, VB, CS, V (inc., man. mark), A (fin. init.), (cat. #847, 1970's)
6) Logo, VB, CS, Original, PG (thrower's init.), (1970's)
(Private Collection)

Plate 353
1) Logo, VB, (late teens-1920)
2) Logo, VB, CS 44 (fin. init.), || (ink man. mark), (cat. #777, 1950's-1960's)
3) Logo, VB, CS, 45 (fin. mark), ||| (ink, man. mark), (cat. #647, mid-1940's to1950's)
4) Logo, VB, CS, (creamer, mid-1940's to 1950's)
5) Logo, VB, CS, L (fin. init.), (sugar, mid-1940's to 1950's)
6) Logo, VB, CS, (mid-1940's to 1950's)
(Private Collection)

Plate 354
1) Logo, VB, CS, F (fin. init.), || (ink, man. mark), (1960's)
2) Logo, VB, SP (fin. init.), (1950's-1960's)
3) Logo, VB, CS, 6 (fin. #), (cat. #468, mid-1940's to 1960's)
4) Logo, VB, CS, A (fin. init.), (sugar, cat. #291 S, 1970's)
5) Logo, VB, CS, P (fin. init.), (cat. #773, mid-1940's to1960's)
6) Logo, VB, CS, S (fin. init.), (creamer, cat. #291 C, 1970's)
(Private Collection)

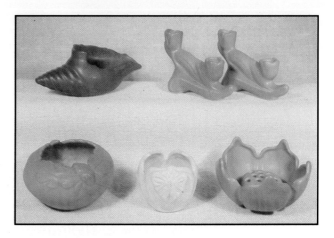

Plate 355
1) Logo, VB, CS, Original, NC (thrower's init.),
   (1950's-1960's)
2) Logo, VB, CS, (cat. #505, mid-1930's to mid-1940's)
3) Logo, VB, CS, Original, O (thrower's init.),
   22 (fin. init.), (1950's)
(Private Collection)

Plate 357
1) Logo, VB, CS, 28 (fin. #), 5 (ink, man. mark),
   (cat. #325 A, late 1940's-1960's)
2) Logo, VB, CS, F (fin. init.),
   (pair, candleholders, cat.#116, 1950's-1960's)
3) Logo, VB, CS, 8 (fin. #), (cat. #734, mid-1940's to 1960's)
4) Logo, VB, CS, K (fin. init.), (#684, 1970-present)
5) Logo, VB, CS, DM (fin. init.), (cat. #151, 1970-present)
(Private Collection)

Plate 358
Logo, VB, CS, (#833, 1920's)
(Private Collection)

Plate 356
1) Logo, VB, CS, 14 (fin. #), (cat. #647,
   mid-1940's to 1950's)
2) Logo, VB, CS, 6 (fin. #), (cat. #43,
   mid-1930's to mid-1940's)
3) Logo, VB, CS, (#645, mid-1930's to mid-1940's)
4) Logo, VB, CS, (#681, mid-1930's to mid-1940's)
5) Logo, (mid-1940's to 1950's)
6) Logo, (mid-1940's to 1950's)
7) Logo, VB, Original, O (thrower's init.), 49
   (fin. init.), (1950's)
(Private Collection)

Plate 359
1) Gold Ore Glaze, CS, (cat. #322, 1956)
2) Gold Ore Glaze, CS, (cat. #468, 1956)
3) Ⓖ by VB, CS, (cat. #325 A, 1956)
4) Ⓖ by VB, CS, (1956)
(Private Collection)

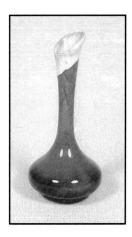

Plate 360
Anna Van Briggle,
CS, (1955-1968)
(Private Collection)

Plate 363
1) Logo, VB, CS, No. 90, special ed., HUN (fin. init.),
   (#17, late 1980's)
2) Logo, VB, CSC, AO (fin. init.),
   (cat. #509, 1980's-present)
3) Logo, VB, CS, No. 68, special ed., LS (fin. init.),
   (#17, late 1980's)
4) Logo, VB, CSC, Original, CS (thrower's init.)
5) Logo, VB, CS, (cat. #684, 1982-1988)
6) Logo, VB, CSC, AO (fin. init.), (cat. #54, late 1980's)
(Van Briggle Art Pottery Company)

Plate 361
Logo, VB, CS, CCB
(Colorado Central Bank), 1971
(Private Collection)

Plate 364
1) Logo, VB, CSC, ⑧⑤ (date), (1985)
2) Logo, VB, CS, ⑧④ (date), (1984)
3) Logo, VB, CSC, AO (fin. init.), (cat.#150, late 1980's)
4) Logo, VB, CS, ⑧⑤ (date), (1985)
5) Logo, VB, CS, MW (fin. init., late 1980's)
(Van Briggle Art Pottery Company)

Plate 362
1) Logo, VB, CS, (1968-1970's)
2) Colo. Lions, 1968, Dallas
3) Logo, VB, CS, DK (fin. init.), (1968-1970's)
(Private Collection)

Plate 365
　1) Logo, VB, CS, HVM (fin. init.), (#128, late 1980's-1991)
　2) Logo, VB, CSC, VR (fin. init.), (#167, late 1980's-1991)
(Private Collection)

Plate 366
　1) Logo, VB, CS, LS (fin. init.), IV (inc. man. mark),
　　(#17, late 1980's)
　2) Logo, VB, CSC, TE (fin. init.), II
　　(inc. man. mark), (#9[?], late 1980's)
　3) Logo, VB, CS, HVM (fin. init.), IV
　　(inc. man. mark), (late 1980's)
(Van Briggle Art Pottery Company)

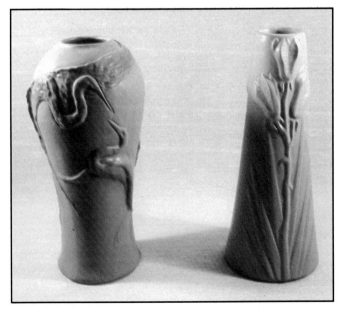

Plate 367
　1) Logo, VB, CS, P (fin. init.), (late 1980's)
　2) Logo, VB, CSC, VR (fin. init.), (#157, late 1980's)
(Van Briggle Art Pottery Company)

Plate 368
  1) Logo, VB, CS, (cat. #509, late 1980's)
  2) Logo, VB, CSC, CF (fin. init.), (late 1980's)
  3) Logo, VB, CS, LS (fin. init.), (late 1980's)
  (Van Briggle Art Pottery Company)

Plate 369
  1) Logo, VB, CS, MK (fin. init.), (cat. #101, late 1980's)
  2) Logo, VB, CS, MB (fin. init.), (cat. #100, late 1980's)
  (Van Briggle Art Pottery Company)

Plate 370
  1) Logo, VB, CS, HVM (fin. init.), (late 1980's-1991)
  2) Logo, VB, CS, MB (fin. init.), (late 1980's-1991)
  3) Logo, VB, CS, MB (fin. init.), (late 1980's-1991)
  (Private Collection)

Plate 371

1) Logo, VB, CS, 2 (fin. init.), (late 1980's)
2) Logo, VB, CS, MB (fin. init.), (cat. #507, late 1980's)
3) Logo, VB, CSC, AO (fin. init.), (cat. #264, late 1980's)
4) Logo, VB, CS, VB (fin. init.), (cat. #19, late 1980's)
5) Logo, VB, CSC, Original, JC (thrower's init.),
   (late 1980's)
6) Logo, VB, CS, MB (fin. init.), (cat. #817, late 1980's)
(Van Briggle Art Pottery Company)

Plate 372

1) Logo, VB, CSC, TE (fin. init.), (#9[?], late 1980's)
2) Logo, VB, CS, AS (fin. init.), (Three Graces, late 1980's)
(Van Briggle Art Pottery Company)

Plate 373

    1) Logo, VB, CSC, ABL (fin. init.), (cat. #470, late 1980's)
    2) Logo, VB, CS, DR (fin. init.), (cat. #505, 1987-1988)
    3) Logo, VB, CS, AMB (fin. init.), (cat. #263, late 1980's)
    4) Logo, VB, CS, CF (fin. init.), (late 1980's)
    5) Logo, VB, CS, AS (fin. init.), (late 1980's)
    6) Logo, VB, CS, LS (fin. init.), (late 1980's)
    (Van Briggle Art Pottery Company)

Plate 374

    1) Logo, VB, CS, AS (fin. init.), (late 1980's)
    2) Logo, VB, CS, AS (fin. init.), (cat. #156, late 1980's)
    (Van Briggle Art Pottery Company)

Plate 375
1) Logo, VB, CSC, MN (fin. init.),
   (cat. #778, late 1980's)
2) Logo, VB, CS, MK (fin. init.),
   (cat. #150, late 1980's)
3) Logo, VB, CSC, AD (fin. init.),
   (cat. #151, late 1980's)
4) Logo, VB, CSC, Original, RF (thrower's init.),
   (late 1980's)
5) Logo, VB, CSC, Original, JC (thrower's init.),
   (late 1980's)
6) Logo, VB, CSC, Original, RF (thrower's init.),
   (late 1980's)
(Van Briggle Art Pottery Company)

Plate 377
1) Logo, VB, CSC, TE (fin. init.),
   (cat. #71, late 1980's)
2) Logo, VB, CSC, TE (fin. init.), (late 1980's)
3) Logo, VB, CSC, ABL (fin. init.), (late 1980's)
4) Logo, VB, CS, DR (fin. init.), (late 1980's)
5) Logo, VB, CS, Original, RH (thrower's init.),
   (late 1980's)
(Van Briggle Art Pottery Company)

Plate 376
1) Logo, VB, CS, DR (fin. init.), (cat. #777, late 1980's)
2) Logo, VB, CSC, AS (fin. init.), III
   (inc. man. mark), (late 1980's)
3) Logo, VB, CSC, AO (fin. init.), IV
   (inc. man. mark), (late 1980's)
(Van Briggle Art Pottery Company)

Plate 378
1) Logo, VB, CSC, AO (fin. init.), (late 1980's)
2) Logo, VB, CSC, CB (fin. init.), (cat. #132, late 1980's)
3) Logo, VB, CSC, UR (fin. init.), (cat. #46, late 1980's)
(Van Briggle Art Pottery Company)

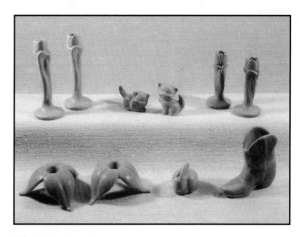

Plate 379

1) Logo, VB, CSC, VR (fin. init.),
   (pair, candlesticks, cat. #CHIB, late 1980's)
2) Logo, VB, CSC, YR (fin. init.),
   (pair, kittens, late 1980's)
3) Logo, VB, CSC, CB (fin. init.),
   (pair, candlesticks, cat. #CHIA, late 1980's)
4) Unmarked, (pair, candleholders, cat. #CS3,
   late 1980's)
5) Logo, VB, CS, AS (fin. init.), (late 1980's)
6) Logo, VB, CS, MB (fin. init.), (late 1980's)
(Van Briggle Art Pottery Company)

Plate 380

1) Logo, VB, CSC, P (fin. init.), (cat. #131, late 1980's)
2) Logo, VB, CSC, CF (fin. init.), (1987-1988)
3) Logo, VB, CSC, CB (fin. init.), (late 1980's)
4) Logo, VB, CS, AS (fin. init.), (1987-1988)
5) Logo, VB, CSC, CF (fin. init.), (late 1980's)
6) Logo, VB, CS, (late 1980's)
(Van Briggle Art Pottery Company)

Plate 381

1) Logo, VB, CS, AS (fin. init.),
   (cat. #325 A, late 1980's)
2) Logo, VB, CSC, CF (fin. init.),
   (cat. #325 B, late 1980's)
3) Logo, VB, CS, MB (fin. init.),
   (cat. #325 C, late 1980's)
(Van Briggle Art Pottery Company)

Chapter VI

Catalogs, Pamphlets, and Post Cards

Throughout its years of operation, the Van Briggle Pottery Company has produced catalogs, pamphlets, and post cards in various formats. Typically these items were used to advertise the numerous products manufactured by the pottery. They are of interest in that they aid in identifying items by their respective design or catalog number, and provide a historic record of merchandise made during various time periods. The following is a small sample of interesting catalogs, pamphlets, and post cards, which are reproduced with permission from the Van Briggle Art Pottery Company.

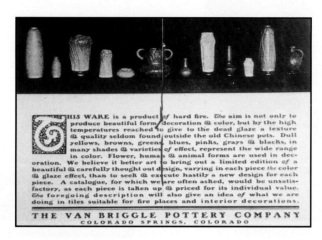

Plate 382
Pamphlet, Early 1900s, Nevada Avenue Plant
(Courtesy of the Denver Public Library, Western
History Department)

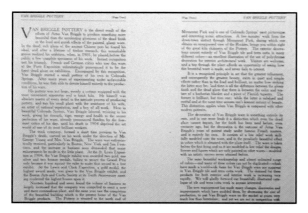

Plate 383

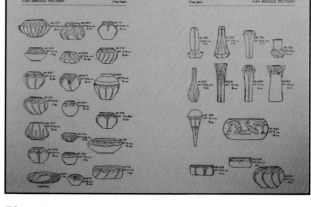

Plate 386

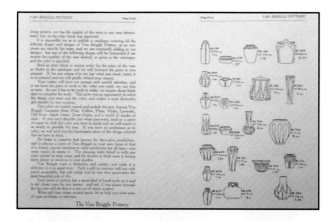

Plate 384

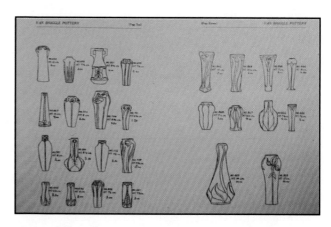

Plate 387

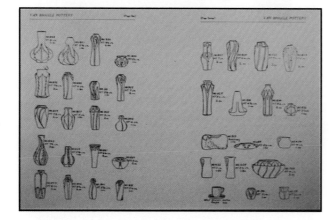

Plate 385

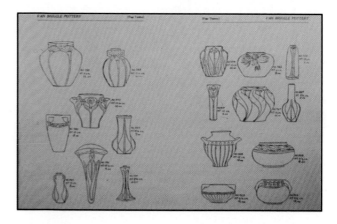

Plate 388

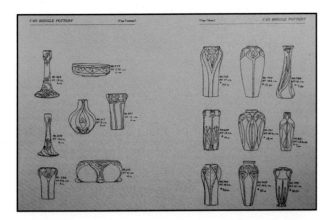

Plate 389

Plates 390 to 398
Catalog, 1920's period
(Courtesy of the Denver Public Library, Western History Department)

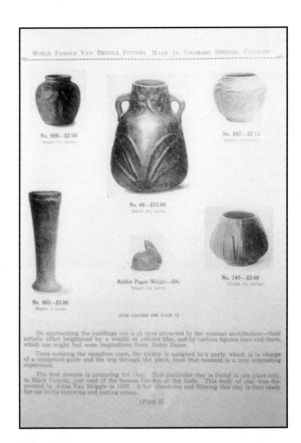

Plate 391

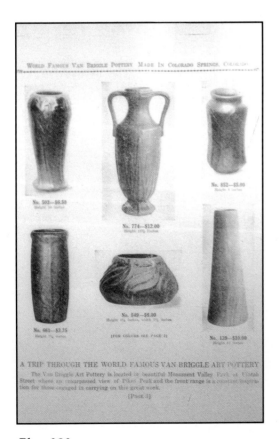

Plate 390

Plate 392

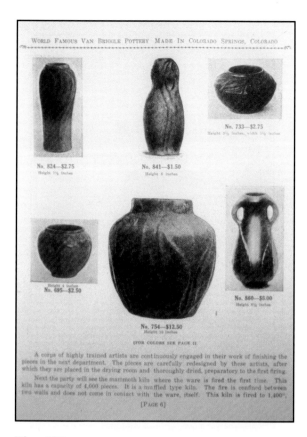

Plate 393

Plate 395

Plate 394

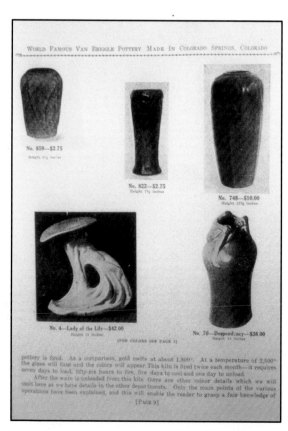

Plate 396

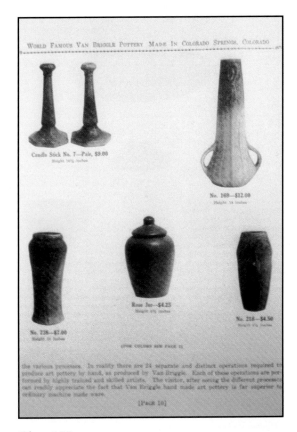

Plate 397

Plate 399

Plate 398

Plates 399 and 400
Pamphlet, 1930's period
(Private Collection)

"Siren of the Sea"

You will marvel at such beauty. "Siren of the Sea", shown above, is only one of the many famous Van Briggle pieces. Such pieces of art are beyond comparison with the mediocre.

Although Van Briggle Art Pottery has received the world's highest awards, it does not take a connoisseur to appreciate its unsurpassed beauty, any more than it takes an artist to appreciate the gorgeous scenery in which the Pikes Peak Region abounds.

Van Briggle Pottery
COLORADO SPRINGS, COLORADO

Plate 401
Pamphlet, 1930's period
(Courtesy of the Denver Public Library, Western History Department)

"THROWING ON THE POTTER'S WHEEL"
[The oldest art in history]

About 2,600 Years Ago, a Great Man Said—

"Then I went down to the potter's house, and, behold, he was making a work on the wheels."—Jer. 18:3.

Is It Not Remarkable

that this ancient art of "throwing on the potter's wheel" is practiced the same today as in the prophet's time?

Is It Not More Remarkable

that people today are just as thrilled, just as inspired, as was Jeremiah 2,600 years ago, when he beheld "throwing on the potter's wheel"?

AS OUR GUEST

You are invited to see this ancient art at the Van Briggle Art Pottery. Courteous, well-informed guides will conduct you through the especially arranged demonstration rooms. The things to be seen are unusual and unique.

THERE IS NO CHARGE THIS TRIP IS FREE

Van Briggle has captured more world exhibit awards than any other art pottery in the world. At the Paris Exhibit in 1900 one piece of Van Briggle art pottery sold for $3,000.

FOR DIRECTIONS, SEE THE MAP ON INSIDE PAGE

Plate 403
Pamphlet, 1930's period
(Courtesy of the Denver Public Library, Western History Department)

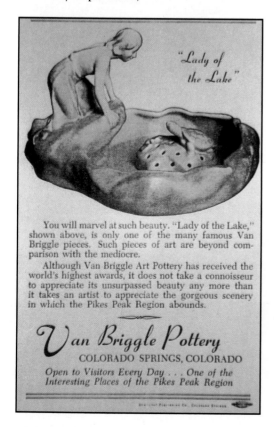

"Lady of the Lake"

You will marvel at such beauty. "Lady of the Lake," shown above, is only one of the many famous Van Briggle pieces. Such pieces of art are beyond comparison with the mediocre.

Although Van Briggle Art Pottery has received the world's highest awards, it does not take a connoisseur to appreciate its unsurpassed beauty any more than it takes an artist to appreciate the gorgeous scenery in which the Pikes Peak Region abounds.

Van Briggle Pottery
COLORADO SPRINGS, COLORADO
Open to Visitors Every Day . . . One of the Interesting Places of the Pikes Peak Region

Plate 402
Pamphlet, 1940's period
(Private Collection)

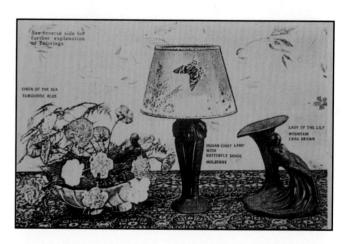

The "SIREN OF THE SEA" is an outstanding Van Briggle Masterpiece. A large sea shell, resting on three small shells with a Mermaid reclining on the edge. Another sea shell forms the flower holder. Height over all 8 inches. Width of shell 15 inches. Price $42.50.

The "LADY OF THE LILY." One of the most artistic conceptions of any American potter. Height 11 inches. Price $42.00.

The "INDIAN CHIEF" lamp with "BUTTERFLY" shade. The real butterflies, flowers and grasses used in producing the unusual effects, are gathered from the four corners of the earth. No word picture could describe the beauty and charm of these wonderful lamps. Height 20 inches. Price $25.50.

WE PREPAY ALL TRANSPORTATION CHARGES AND GUARANTEE SAFE DELIVERY. Gifts shipped direct to recipients when desired. Any Van Briggle piece may be had in any of the three colorings.

VAN BRIGGLE ART POTTERY CO.   COLORADO SPRINGS, COLO.
(At the foot of Pikes Peak)

Plates 404 and 405
Advertising card, 1920's period
(Courtesy of the Colorado Springs Pioneers Museum)

Catalogs, Pamphlets, And Post Cards 119

Plate 406
Post card, Memorial Pottery Plant, teens period
(Private Collection)

Plate 409
Catalog, early teens period, E.D. Curtis era
(Courtesy of Special Collections, Tutt
Library, Colorado College)

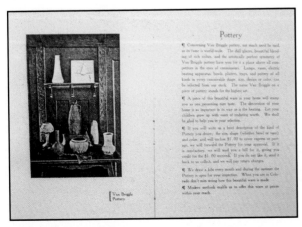

Plate 407
Post card, Memorial Pottery Plant, 1920's period
(Private Collection)

Plate 410
Catalog, early teens period, E.D. Curtis era
(Courtesy of Special Collections, Tutt Library,
Colorado College)

Plate 408
Catalog, early teens period, E. D. Curtis era
(Courtesy of Special Collections, Tutt Library,
Colorado College)

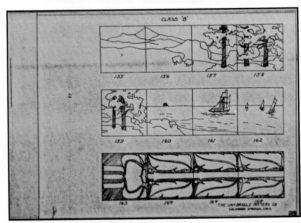

Plate 411
Tile plans, period unknown (Pre-1920's)
(Courtesy of Special Collections, Tutt Library, Colorado
College)

Glossary

Anna Van Pottery   Pottery utilizing a high gloss glaze (Honey Brown, Trout Lake Green, and Jet Black) made to commemorate Anne Van Briggle Ritter. These pieces were not signed by Anne as sometimes believed. Undersides lack the logo but display "Anna Van" or "Anna Van Briggle" alone or with "Colo. Spgs." This mark was used from 1955 through 1968; the standard format of marking was resumed in 1968 and has been utilized to the present day.

Arabic Number   Code related to the manufacturing process, usually occurring as a two-digit incised number, occasionally found on early dated pieces.

Art Pottery Line   Pottery produced by the Van Briggle Company between 1900 and 1912. Design numbers which range from 1 to 904 were assigned to each piece. These numbers are listed in Robert Wyman Newton's "Catalogue of Van Briggle Designs."

Artist Mark   Specific mark or scribe (e.g., ⋁⤬, ⊂⊃ , ⑥) incised on the undersides of early dated pottery, representing the individual responsible for the finishing, etching, or manufacture of the item.

Artist Signature   Incised signature of the individual responsible for creating or throwing a particular piece of pottery.

Beige Bottom   A beige or light tan colored underside which usually has a coating of clear shellac. Produced from 1970 to the present.

Block Lettering   Incised capital letters indicating the company name and city of manufacture (VAN BRIGGLE, CoLo. SPGS.). Characteristic of items produced before the mid-1930's.

Catalog Number   Number assigned to pottery usually produced after 1920, which is listed in company catalogs and pamphlets. These numbers are different from the early design numbers, and were never marked on the pottery itself.

Colorado Springs   Company manufacturing location, incised on the undersides of pottery, in capital (block), small, script, and written letters, in various combinations, depending on the period of production. Usually occurs in an abbreviated form (e.g., Colo. Spgs.).

Design Number   Specific number ranging from 1 through 904 in Robert Wyman Newton's Catalog of Van Briggle Designs. These numbers relate to particular patterns which are part of the art pottery line. Numbers were either incised or die-stamped. A letter which

	follows the design number indicates a variation in the pattern size.
Die-stamped	Result of a process by which marks, letters, and design numbers are stamped or impressed into the clay.
Dirty Bottom	Term coined by Robert Wyman Newton, used to describe undersides which contain glaze streaks and residue, giving a dirty appearance as if they were wiped off after glazing. Clay colors are usually dark tan, red, cream, or lighter gray. Typically occurred during the late teens to 1920.
Experimental Glaze Roman Numeral	Codes for experimental glaze color, written in ink, usually occurring on pottery produced from 1902 through 1904.
Finisher Initial	Incised initial or initials, usually representing the individual who was responsible for etching or finishing the item once removed from the mold, or the individual who created the item (Original).
Finisher Number	Numbers related to the manufacturing process which represent the individual responsible for etching or finishing the item after it is removed from the mold.
Gold Ore Glaze	Glaze produced for a short period during 1956 utilizing mill tailings from the gold mines at Cripple Creek, Colorado. Glaze has a red speckled, light tan color. Undersides lack the logo and display an incised G or "Gold Ore Glaze."
Hand Carved	Incised on the undersides of pottery which are etched or carved with designs. Usually accompanied by the artist's initial.
Incised	Process by which marks, letters, design numbers, and writings are etched into the clay by hand.
Ink Mark	An ink slash, dash, or number related to the manufacturing process, found on pottery made usually after the mid-1930's.
Logo	Trademark of Van Briggle pottery, ▨ an incised double "A" in a square, signifying the initials of Artus and Anne Van Briggle, found on almost all pottery, excluding some specialty lines.
Original	Appears on the undersides of pottery which was hand thrown. Usually accompanied by the artist's signature or initials.
Residue Bottom	Underside which appears to have the remains of glaze and residue left from the manufacturing process. Should not be mistaken for a "dirty bottom," as residue bottoms clearly evidence a white clay. Items probably were produced from the early 1930's through the mid-1940's. Some undersides may have a coating of shellac.
Roman Numeral	Mark which indicates type of clay used, usually incised on undersides from 1901 through 1905. Present day items may also have small incised Roman numerals which relate to the manufacturing process.

Sandy Bottom	Underside which appears to have a sandy toned color with a grainy texture, sometimes called a "buff bottom," and produced during the 1920's.
U.S.A.	Incised on the undersides of pottery which was produced and exported from 1922 through 1926.
Van Briggle	Company name incised on most items in capital (block), small, script, and written letters, in various combinations, depending on the period of production.
White Bottom	Generally, an underside with a clean, white appearance, and a clear coating of shellac. These pieces were produced utilizing a white clay, and appear to have been made from the mid-1940's through the late 1960's.

Notes

[1]"Colorado Springs: The Home of Van Briggle Pottery," *Colorado Springs Gazette*, January 1905, New Year Edition, p. 65.

[2]George D. Galloway, "The Van Briggle Pottery," *Colorado Springs Gazette*, 25 August 1901, p. 10.

[3]Ibid., p. 10.

[4]"Colorado Roundup," *Denver Times*, 21 February 1902.

[5]"World Has Lost a Genius," *Colorado Springs Gazette*, 6 July 1904.

[6]Frank H. Riddle, "The New Pottery and Art Terra Cotta Plant of the Van Briggle Pottery Company at Colorado Springs, Colo.," *Transactions of the American Ceramic Society*, X (1908), 5.

[7]"Fire Wreaks Havoc at Van Briggle Pottery," *Colorado Springs Gazette*, 25 June 1919, pp. 2-3.

[8]"Flood Tops Six-Foot Wall at Van Briggle," *Colorado Springs Gazette*, 31 May 1935.

[9]Galloway, p. 10.

[10]George D. Galloway, "The Van Briggle Pottery," *Brush and Pencil*, IX, No. 1 (1901), 8.

[11]Riddle, pp . 7-9.

[12]Irene Sargent, "Chinese Pots and Modern Faience," *The Craftsman*, IV, No. VI (1903).

[13]Robert Wyman Newton, Letter to authors, 14 May 1991.

References

Berberian, Rosalie M. *Guide for Dating Van Briggle Pottery*. New Haven, CT: ARK Antiques, 1978.

Bogue, Dorothy McGraw. *The Van Briggle Story*. 2nd ed. Century One Press, 1976.

Bowdoin, W. G. "Some American Pottery Forms." *The Art Interchange*. April, 1903, pp. 87-90.

Colorado Springs Gazette. 25 August 1901, 7 December 1901, 8 August 1902, 12 May 1903, 1 January 1904, Annual Edition January 1904, 5 July 1904, 6 July 1904, New Year Edition January 1905, 24 February 1905, 14 July 1906, 25 October 1907, 16 February 1908, 15 July 1908, 22 November 1908, 3 December 1908, 4 December 1908, 22 December 1908, 25 June 1919, 20 April 1920, 6 August 1920, 8 December 1922, 7 December 1924, 16 November 1929, 31 May 1935.

Colorado Springs Gazette Telegraph. 15 May 1955, 8 December 1968, 21 May 1967, 17 May 1970, 19 January 1975, 15 October 1979, 28 March 1982, 14 August 1982.

Crouch, Lois K., Researcher/Historian on Van Briggle Pottery, Colorado Springs, CO. Personal interview. February, 1990.

Denver Republican. 15 June 1902, 14 December 1912.

Denver Times. 12 January 1902.

Galloway, George D. "The Van Briggle Pottery." *Brush and Pencil*, IX, No. 1 (Oct. 1901), pp. 1-8.

Gibson, Paul. Former employee, Van Briggle Art Pottery Company, Colorado Springs, CO. Personal interview. April, 1990.

I. H. W. "General Art Notes." *Fine Arts Journal*, XIV, No. 6 (June 1903), pp. 235-237.

Mangus, Darlynn. Office Manager, Van Briggle Art Pottery Company, Colorado Springs, CO. Letter to authors. 18 April 1991.

Nelson, Scott H. Author, "A Collector's Guide to Van Briggle Pottery," Santa Fe, NM. Letter to authors. 6 June 1991.

Nelson, Scott H., Lois K. Crouch, Euphemia B. Demmin, and Robert Wyman Newton. *A Collector's Guide to Van Briggle Pottery*. Indiana, PA: A. G. Halldin Publishing Co., Inc., 1986. Provides an excellent and detailed review of the history of Van Briggle throughout its years of operation, as well as discussing dating and listing the various designs.

Newton, Robert Wyman. "Catalogue of Van Briggle Designs." In *A Collector's Guide to Van Briggle Pottery*. Scott H. Nelson, et al. Indiana, PA: A. G. Halldin Publishing Co., Inc., 1986.

Riddle, Frank H. "The New Pottery and Art Terra Cotta Plant of the Van Briggle Pottery Company at Colorado Springs, Colo." *Transactions of the American Ceramic Society*, X (1908), pp. 3-13.

Ruge, Clara. "American Ceramics: A Brief Review of Progress." *International Studio*, XXVIII (March 1906), pp. 21-28.

Sargent, Irene. "Chinese Pots and Modern Faience." *The Craftsman*, IV, No. IV (Sept. 1903), pp. 415-425.

Smithsonian Institution. Division of Ceramics and Glass, Washington, DC. Letter to authors. 6 March 1990.

Stellwagen, Lois. Employee, Van Briggle Art Pottery Company, Colorado Springs, CO. Personal interview. June, 1990.

Stevenson, Bertha. Van Briggle Art Pottery Company, Colorado Springs, CO. Letter to authors. 7 January 1991.

Stevenson, Kenneth W. Owner-Manager, Van Briggle Art Pottery Company, Colorado Springs, CO. Letter to authors. 8 September 1990.

Stevenson, Kenneth W. Owner-Manager, Van Briggle Art Pottery Company, Colorado Springs, CO. Personal interview. March, 1990.

Sturgis, Russell. "The Field of Art." *Scribner's Magazine*, XXXII, No. 5 (Nov. 1902), pp. 635-640.

Swaim, Connie. "Van Briggle Pottery Still Producing Old Line." *Antique Week*, 20, No. 43 (Feb. 1, 1968), pp. 1 and 32.

Taylor, Ralph C. *Pueblo Star-Journal and Sunday Chieftan*. 12 June 1955.

Van Briggle Art Pottery Company. Company pamphlets, handouts, and paperwork. Early 1900's to the present.

"Van Briggle Adds to Colorado's Fame." *Glass and Pottery World*, No. 4 (April 1908), pp. 15-16.

Van Briggle Pottery: The Early Years. Colorado Springs Fine Arts Center, Colorado Springs, CO, 1975. (Barbara M. Arnest, Editor; Robert E. Morris, Editorial Associate; Robert Wyman Newton, The Catalogue; Lois K. Crouch and Euphemia B. Demmin, Research Associates.)

Wills, Fred. Master Potter, Van Briggle Art Pottery Company, Retired. Colorado Springs, CO. Personal interview. June, 1990.

Index To Plates

Item/Design Number	Plate Number	Item/Design Number	Plate Number
#340D	201	#501	212
#343	283	#503	299, 343
#348	196	#507	251
#349C	245	#509	277
#349D	256	#510	200, 209, 312
#350	250	#521	182
#352	256	#522	317, 347
#361	201	#527	173
#364	264	#535	197, 294
#365	205	#540	294
#371	189	#544	277, 300
#373	267	#548	172
#378	176	#549	283
#379	292	#553	222
#380	269	#568	278
#381	299	#576	278
#382	182, 220	#579	222
#384	202, 266	#589	231, 306
#385	203, 281	#591	251, 266
#387	200, 254	#594	199
#390	174	#595	182, 278
#393	279	#597	256
#397	268	#601	173
#398	301, 318	#606	220
#400	97	#608	175, 314
#402	293	#613	219
#405	238	#614	263
#406	254	#617	199
#410	211	#619	213
#411	271	#622	113, 121
#415	220	#623	120
#420B	267	#626	280
#422	282	#631	201, 231
#425	226	#632	192
#430	297	#633	159
#435	217	#635	295
#436	209	#636	220, 284
#450	228	#639	274
#452	264	#644	262
#453	182	#645	189, 222, 298, 318, 320, 356
#454	187		
#456	182, 204	#646	221, 279
#460	269	#647	233
#464	177	#648	216
#469D	213	#649	249, 268, 293
#470C	184	#650	98, 188
#470D	187	#651	173, 258
#476	240	#653	199
#480	231	#654	181, 258, 307
#482A	261	#661	252, 317
#486	221	#664	195, 226
#490	262	#665	269
#496	193	#666	257

Item/Design Number	Plate Number	Item/Design Number	Plate Number
#670	234	#782	208
#671	182, 318	#786	244, 259
#674	232	#787	204, 236
#676	245	#788	178
#677	245	#792	199, 322, 344
#678	301, 309	#794	323
#681	215, 321, 347, 356	#795	294
#683	245, 345, 347	#797	254
#685	210	#798	202
#688	210, 231, 298, 301, 310, 342	#800	175
		#806	271
#693	264	#808	227
#694	222, 226, 229	#820	218
#695	297, 299	#821	187
#696	240, 280, 292, 297	#822	177, 228, 341, 344
#698	222, 333	#824	185, 310, 321, 322
#700	343	#832	253
#702	217	#833	231, 295, 320, 323, 324, 358
#709	177, 207, 262		
#719	219, 265	#834	232, 347
#721	238, 296	#837	228, 318, 341
#722	326	#838	229, 305
#726	254	#840	298
#727	217	#841	323, 342, 344
#728	210	#843	309
#729	244	#847	299
#733	310	#849	210, 305
#733C	298	#851	324
#734	271	#852	305, 326, 322
#735	299, 306	#857	307
#737	276, 279	#858	301, 319, 346
#738	310, 315, 318	#859	255, 305, 323, 343
#742	195	#860	309, 310
#747	297, 321, 324, 341	#861	258
#748	244, 311	#863	228, 301, 319, 341
#749	230	#869	246
#750	187	#875	96
#753	274	#880	254
#754	186, 303, 304	#890	227
#756	214	#902	302
#757	181	#903	271, 312, 316
#761	210	#903D	312, 314, 319
#762	200, 272, 276	#903E	316
#763	285		
#763E	158	Figurals	
#766	206, 235		
#768	241	Anna Van	78
#770	228	Corn Grinding Maiden	369, 370
#772	193, 251	Daydreamer	73
#774	339, 340	Hopi Maiden	76
#776	306, 312	Indian Busts	80, 81
#780	178, 309	Indian Chief	143, 144, 145, 366
#781	317	Lady of the Lake	74

Price Guide

Prices for Van Briggle pottery are determined by a variety of factors such as: 1) condition (e.g., cracks, chips, hairline cracks, and repairs), 2) year or period of manufacture, 3) size and shape, 4) glaze color or combinations of glaze color, and 5) type, clarity, and detail of designs and patterns. It is also important to remember that prices appear to vary according to geographical area, and that the price an individual is willing to pay for an item may override any set pricing guidelines.

Each piece of pottery encountered by the authors displayed unique characteristics in terms of glaze color, shading, tone, and clarity of design. This was particularly true of early dated pottery (pre-1913). Replications of similar design and color appear to have been more common during the late teens, increasing in frequency throughout the later years of production (1920s to the present). Therefore, the merit of each piece of pottery in light of these characteristics is also an important consideration when pricing items.

The prices listed here are intended to serve as a guide and were based on dealer, auction, flea market, and collector estimates. Further, prices may not reflect the estimates of the owners (individual or organization). It was not uncommon for the authors to encounter similar pieces within a wide price range. Prices are listed according to individual plate numbers and are read from top row, left to right, and bottom row, left to right.

Plate 69	$6,000 – $6,500	Plate 83	$850 – $1,000
Plate 70	$1,000 – $1,250	Plate 84	$225 – $275
Plate 71	$300 – $350	Plate 85	$1,750 – $2,000
Plate 72	$425 – $475	Plate 86	$1,500 – $1,650
Plate 73	$275 – $325	Plate 87	$600 – $750
Plate 74	$400 – $475 (with flower frog)	Plate 89	$38,000 – $42,000
Plate 75	$400 – $450	Plate 90	$14,000 – $17,000 (crack)
Plate 76	$150 – $175	Plate 91	$800 – $1,000
Plate 77	$225 – $250	Plate 92	$900 – $1,100
Plate 78	$400 – $475	Plate 94	$7,000 – $8,500
Plate 79	$65 – $90	Plate 95	$1,000 – $1,350
Plate 80	1) $325 – $400 2) $275 – $325 3) $350 – $400	Plate 96	$2,200 – $2,500
		Plate 97	$2,000 – $2,500 (without shade)
Plate 81	1) $300 – $350 2) $350 – $400 3) $325 – $375	Plate 98	$4,500 – $5,000 (without shade)
		Plate 99	$450 – $500
Plate 82	$8,500 – $10,000	Plate 100	$300 – $375

Plate 101	$450 – $525	
Plate 102	$350 – $400 (without shade)	
Plate 103	$150 – $225 (without shade)	
Plate 104	$375 – $450 (without shade)	
Plate 105	$375 – $450	
Plate 106	$90 – $135	
Plate 107	$75 – $125	
Plate 108	$100 – $175	
Plate 109	$100 – $175	
Plate 110	$1,750 – $2,000	
Plate 111	$600 – $700	
Plate 112	$1,600 – $1,800	
Plate 113	$425 – $525	
Plate 114	$425 – $525	
Plate 115	1) $575 – $650	
	2) $600 – $675	
Plate 116	$1,250 – $1,550	
Plate 117	$1,300 – $1,600	
Plate 118	$425 – $525	
Plate 119	$675 – $800	
Plate 120	$525 – $650	
Plate 121	$425 – $525	
Plate 122	$775 – $875 (damaged)	
Plate 125	$550 – $700	
Plate 126	$700 – $850	
Plate 127	1) $230 – $260	
	2) $450 – $500	
	3) $650 – $750	

Plate 128	1) $275 – $325	
	2) $500 – $650	
	3) $500 – $600	
Plate 129	1) $525 – $575	
	2) $650 – $750	
	3) $750 – $850	
Plate 130	1) $375 – $425	
	2) $425 – $500	
	3) $400 – $475	
Plate 131	1) $350 – $400	
	2) $475 – $550	
	3) $425 – $475	
Plate 132	1) $525 – $625	
	2) $525 – $625	
Plate 133	1) $550 – $650	
	2) $500 – $550	
	3) $750 – $875	
Plate 134	$275 – $325	
Plate 135	$350 – $425	
Plate 136	$625 – $725	
Plate 140	1) $750 – $875	
	2) $500 – $600	
Plate 141	$800 – $1,000	
Plate 143	$2,000 – $2,500	
Plate 144	$500 – $600	
Plate 145	$300 – $450	
Plate 146	$350 – $450 (pair)	
Plate 147	$250 – $300 (pair)	
Plate 148	$300 – $375 (pair)	
Plate 149	$400 – $500 (pair)	
Plate 150	$175 – $225 (pair)	
Plate 151	1) $250 – $350	
	2) $200 – $300	

Plate 152	$350 – $450
Plate 153	$450 – $575
Plate 154	$475 – $600
Plate 155	$725 – $775
Plate 156	$200 – $250
Plate 157	$75 – $125 (each)
Plate 158	$450 – $525
Plate 159	$2,250 – $2,750
Plate 160	$400 – $500
Plate 161	$225 – $300

Plate 162
1) $150 – $225
2) $150 – $225

Plate 163
1) $50 – $90
2) $50 – $90

Plate 164
1) $375 – $475
2) $275 – $325

Plate 165
1) $45 – $65
2) $10 – $25
3) $45 – $65
4) $225 – $275
5) $50 – $75
6) $50 – $75

Plate 166
1) $300 – $400
2) $100 – $175

Plate 167 $275 – $325

Plate 168 Undetermined

Plate 169 $425 – $525

Plate 170 $375 – $475

Plate 171 $150 – $225

Plate 172
1) $1,850 – $2,250
2) $525 – $625
3) $425 – $525
4) $500 – $600

5) $850 – $1,000
6) $750 – $850

Plate 173
1) $525 – $575
2) $625 – $700
3) $1,750 – $2,000
4) $675 – $775
5) $350 – $425
6) $650 – $700
7) $275 – $325
8) $725 – $825

Plate 174
1) $1,750 – $1,950
2) $1,350 – $1,500

Plate 175
1) $1,750 – $2,000
2) $725 – $775
3) $475 – $575
4) $1,200 – $1,400

Plate 176 $875 – $925

Plate 177
1) $525 – $575
2) $250 – $325
3) $350 – $450
4) $200 – $250
5) $350 – $400
6) $150 – $225

Plate 178
1) $200 – $275
2) $450 – $600
3) $225 – $300

Plate 179
1) $1,400 – $1,550
2) $800 – $850
3) $1,300 – $1,500
4) $700 – $750
5) $1,200 – $1,350
6) $550 – $600

Plate 180 $13,000 – $17,000

Plate 181
1) $100 – $150
2) $375 – $425
3) $325 – $375

Plate 182
1) $775 – $925
2) $1,200 – $1,350
3) $575 – $675
4) $600 – $700
5) $575 – $650
6) $575 – $675

Plate 183	$650 – $700		Plate 197	1) $975 – $1,200
				2) $400 – $500
Plate 184	1) $725 – $775			3) $1,300 – $1,500
	2) $775 – $825			4) $450 – $525
	3) $350 – $425 (hairline)			5) $350 – $400
				6) $975 – $1,075
Plate 185	1) $10,000 – $13,000			
	2) $35,000 – $40,000		Plate 198	1) $2,000 – $2,300
	3) $275 – $350			2) $925 – $1,050
	4) $20,000 – $24,000			
	5) $800 – $875		Plate 199	1) $3,000 – $4,500
				2) $725 – $775
Plate 186	1) $1,500 – $1,700			3) $3,500 – $4,500
	2) $1,300 – $1,500			4) $225 – $275
				5) $750 – $850
Plate 187	1) $1,000 – $1,200			6) $275 – $325
	2) $750 – $800			
	3) $1,000 – $1,200		Plate 200	1) $1,800 – $2,200
	4) $725 – $800			2) $1,100 – $1,300
	5) $1,750 – $2,000			3) $650 – $750
Plate 188	1) $5,000 – $7,500		Plate 201	1) $1,100 – $1,250
	2) $1,550 – $1,750			2) $900 – $1,000
				3) $1,350 – $1,500
Plate 189	1) $625 – $725			4) $675 – $775
	2) $325 – $375			5) $800 – $900
	3) $925 – $1,000			6) $625 – $700
	4) $350 – $400			
	5) $925 – $1,000		Plate 202	1) $1,600 – $1,850
	6) $450 – $500			2) $550 – $650
Plate 190	$475 – $550		Plate 203	1) $1,200 – $1,300
				2) $1,750 – $1,900
Plate 191	1) $425 – $525			3) $1,500 – $1,700
	2) $6,500 – $8,000			
	3) $625 – $725		Plate 204	1) $775 – $875
				2) $1,850 – $2,000
Plate 192	$1,800 – $2,000			3) $550 – $625
Plate 193	1) $775 – $900		Plate 205	1) $4,000 – $6,500
	2) $1,500 – $1,600			2) $1,400 – $1,500
	3) $900 – $1,000			3) $1,200 – $1,450
				4) $500 – $550
Plate 194	$2,500 – $2,800			5) $925 – $975
				6) $775 – $875
Plate 195	1) $1,200 – $1,400			
	2) $225 – $325		Plate 206	$3,000 – $3,300
	3) $875 – $925			
	4) $4,250 – $4,750		Plate 207	1) $75 – $125
	5) $875 – $975			2) $375 – $400
				3) $1,300 – $1,400
Plate 196	$1,600 – $1,750			

Plate 208   1) $375 – $450
                2) $150 – $200

Plate 209   1) $725 – $775
                2) $800 – $875
                3) $250 – $300

Plate 210   1) $225 – $300
                2) $525 – $575
                3) $1,100 – $1,300
                4) $825 – $875
                5) $325 – $375
                6) $300 – $375

Plate 211   1) $2,250 – $2,750
                2) $2,900 – $3,350

Plate 212 $1,100 – $1,250

Plate 213   1) $775 – $850
                2) $425 – $500
                3) $1,100 – $1,250
                4) $1,200 – $1,300
                5) $1,550 – $1,700
                6) $600 – $650

Plate 214   1) $1,350 – $1,500
                2) $3,000 – $4,000

Plate 215   1) $1,400 – $1,700
                2) $2,800 – $3,400
                3) $225 – $300

Plate 216 $1,850 – $2,000

Plate 217   1) $3,000 – $3,500
                2) $2,500 – $2,850
                3) $575 – $625 (lid missing)
                4) $10,000 – $12,000
                5) $425 – $500
                6) $650 – $675

Plate 218   1) $375 – $400
                2) $350 – $425

Plate 219   1) $1,900 – $2,450
                2) $350 – $425

Plate 220   1) $750 – $800
                2) $625 – $675
                3) $600 – $650
                4) $675 – $750
                5) $1,100 – $1,250
                6) $650 – $750

Plate 221   1) $625 – $700
                2) $725 – $775

Plate 222   1) $800 – $875
                2) $650 – $725
                3) $725 – $825
                4) $350 – $425
                5) $1,000 – $1,200
                6) $375 – $475

Plate 223 $475 – $550

Plate 224 $2,700 – $3,300

Plate 225   1) $2,100 – $2,300
                2) $4,500 – $5,000
                3) $2,500 – $2,950

Plate 226   1) $875 – $925
                2) $950 – $1,100
                3) $775 – $875

Plate 227   1) $300 – $375
                2) $425 – $525

Plate 228   1) $200 – $275
                2) $75 – $125
                3) $200 – $275
                4) $175 – $250
                5) $775 – $875
                6) $275 – $350

Plate 229   1) $325 – $400
                2) $975– $1,200
                3) $550 – $675

Plate 230   1) $1,750 – $2,400
                2) $2,700 – $3,500

Plate 231   1) $1,100 – $1,375
                2) $350 – $450
                3) $675 – $725
                4) $550 – $600
                5) $525 – $600
                6) $525 – $550
                7) $375 – $425
                8) $300 – $350

Plate 232   1) $450 – $575
                2) $350 – $400
                3) $225 – $275

Plate 233	1) $1,300 – $1,500	Plate 247	1) $450 – $550
	2) $575 – $675		2) $1,700 – $1,900
Plate 234	1) $12,500 – $15,000	Plate 248	1) $425 – $500
	2) $875 – $1,000		2) $400 – $500
	3) $800 – $850		
	4) $250 – $325	Plate 249	1) $1,250 – $1,550
			2) $2,900 – $3,250
Plate 235	1) $275 – $325		3) $1,300 – $1,500
	2) $1,750 – $2,250		
		Plate 250	1) $1,200 – $1,400
Plate 236	1) $2,000 – $2,300		2) $3,250 – $3,750
	2) $700 – $825		3) $3,150 – $3,650
Plate 237	1) $300 – $375	Plate 251	1) $225 – $275
	2) $375 – $450		2) $650 – $700
	3) $250 – $325		3) $375 – $475
Plate 238	1) $2,750 – $3,300	Plate 252	1) $275 – $375
	2) $1,900 – $2,300		2) $775 – $850
			3) $3,500 – $4,200
Plate 239	1) $3,750 – $4,500		4) $200 – $275 (lid/handle missing)
	2) $1,550 – $1,950		5) $800 – $900
	3) $1,450 – $1,750		6) $550 – $650
Plate 240	1) $575 – $725	Plate 253	1) $125 – $175
	2) $1,950 – $2,350		2) $475 – $550
	3) $2,000 – $2,400		3) $75 – $135
	4) $1,700 – $1,900		
	5) $750 – $875	Plate 254	1) $475 – $550 (lid missing)
	6) $875 – $950		2) $300 – $375
			3) $1,350 – $1,650
Plate 241	$1,900 – $2,100		4) $350 – $425
			5) $1,650 – $2,000
Plate 242	$4,400 – $4,750		
		Plate 255	1) $275 – $375
Plate 243	1) $625 – $675		2) $1,500 – $1,800
	2) $4,700 – $5,400		
	3) $425 – $500	Plate 256	1) $525 – $600
			2) $775 – $875
Plate 244	1) $250 – $325		3) $575 – $650
	2) $275 – $375		4) $550 – $600
	3) $175 – $275		
		Plate 257	1) $800 – $9050
Plate 245	1) $625 – $700		2) $900 – $1,000
	2) $1,300 – $1,550		
	3) $1,200 – $1,300	Plate 258	1) $325 – $400
	4) $275 – $350		2) $2,600 – $3,350
	5) $275 – $350		3) $1,300 – $1,500
	6) $75 – $135		4) $575 – $675
			5) $1,000 – $1,300
Plate 246	1) $375 – $450		6) $375 – $500
	2) $275 – $375		7) $325 – $375

Plate 259   1) $1,750 – $2,000
            2) $2,500 – $2,900
            3) $1,300 – $1,500

Plate 260 $2,250 – $2,700

Plate 261 $850 – $900

Plate 262   1) $1,100 – $1,300
            2) $1,900 – $2,400
            3) $900 – $975
            4) $875 – $925
            5) $825 – $875
            6) $375 – $450

Plate 263   1) $300 – $375
            2) $450 – $500

Plate 264   1) $475 – $575
            2) $800 – $925
            3) $700 – $775
            4) $375 – $450
            5) $575 – $625
            6) $700 – $800

Plate 265   1) $1,850 – $2,200
            2) $3,750 – $4,750

Plate 266   1) $875 – $1,000
            2) $1,100 – $1,350 (manufacturing defect)
            3) $1,750 – $2,000

Plate 267   1) $575 – $675
            2) $1,650 – $1,900
            3) $625 – $675
            4) $875 – $975

Plate 268   1) $1,200 – $1,350
            2) $875 – $950
            3) $1,350 – $1,750

Plate 269   1) $1,200 – $1,350
            2) $850 – $900
            3) $725 – $775
            4) $800 – $900
            5) $1,850 – $2,250

Plate 270 $38,000 – $43,500

Plate 271   1) $325 – $400
            2) $475 – $525
            3) $250 – $275
            4) $575 – $650

            5) $325 – $400 (with flower frog)
            6) $225 – $250

Plate 272 $1,400 – $1,750

Plate 273 $425 – $500

Plate 274   1) $975 – $1,350
            2) $1,200 – $1,400
            3) $925 – $1,050
            4) $2,450 – $2,900
            5) $975 – $950

Plate 275   1) $900 – $1,000
            2) $600 – $675
            3) $2,500 – $2,650

Plate 276   1) $2,700 – $3,500 (flake)
            2) $900 – $1,000
            3) $375 – $425

Plate 277   1) $550 – $600
            2) $500 – $550
            3) $475 – $525

Plate 278   1) $1,200 – $1,400
            2l $3,900 – $4,400
            3) $500 – $550
            4) $200 – $225
            5) $600 – $675

Plate 279   1) $1,300 – $1,450
            2) $627 – $725
            3) $1,350 – $1,500

Plate 280   1) $1,750 – $1,950
            2) $1,800 – $2,000

Plate 281   1) $975 – $1,150
            2) $1,300 – $1,750
            3) $1,700 – $1,900
            4) $1,300 – $1,550
            5) $1,950 – $2,400
            6) $1,200 – $1,400

Plate 282   1) $1,150 – $1,475
            2) $775 – $875

Plate 283   1) $700 – $825
            2) $1,200 – $1,400
            3) $1,250 – $1,500
            4) $1,100 – $1,400
            5) $700 – $775
            6) $1,300 – $1,500

Plate 284	1) $1,000 – $1,350 2) $5,500 – $8,000 3) $2,000 – $2,750	Plate 297	1) $575 – $625 2) $300 – $350 3) $625 – $675 4) $75 – $150 5) $325 – $425 6) $175 – $250
Plate 285	1) $375 – $425 2) $1,500 – $1,600		
Plate 286	1) $650 – $675 2) $575 – $625	Plate 298	1) $175 – $250 2) $750 – $850 3) $300 – $375 4) $875 – $975 5) $275 – $325
Plate 287	$325 – $400		
Plate 288	1) $550 – $625 2) $300 – $350	Plate 299	1) $1,450 – $1,750 2) $250 – $300 3) $875 – $1,000 4) $175 – $250 5) $275 – $375 6) $175 – $250
Plate 289	1) $875 – $925 2) $775 – $825 3) $225 – $275 (damaged)		
Plate 290	1) $300 – $350 2) $525 – $600 3) $425 – $475	Plate 300	1) $75 – $150 2) $450 – $550
Plate 291	1) $3,000 – $4,000 2) $3,300 – $4,100	Plate 301	1) $225 – $300 2) $375 – $475 3) $225 – $300 4) $50 – $90 5) $225 – $300 6) $75 – $140
Plate 292	1) $2,250 – $3,000 2) $3,750 – $4,250 3) $1,300 – $1,500 4) $725 – $775 5) $1,400 – $1,600 6) $875 – $925		
Plate 293	1) $1,900 – $2,300 2) $1,700 – $1,900 3) $875 – $950	Plate 302	1) $250 – $325 2) $250 – $325 3) $250 – $325
Plate 294	1) $1,300 – $1,500 2) $1,450 – $1,700 3) $2,950 – $3,500 4) $950 – $1,100 5) $1,150 – $1,350	Plate 303	1) $450 – $525 2) $175 – $250 3) $550 – $650
		Plate 304	$350 – $425
Plate 295	1) $1,100 – $1,250 2) $350 – $450 3) $1,250 – $1,500 4) $1,900 – $2,150 5) $825 – $925 6) $900 – $1,000	Plate 305	1) $275 – $350 2) $550 – $650 3) $225 – $300 4) $225 – $275 5) $275 – $350 6) $225 – $275
		Plate 306	1) $150 – $200 2) $225 – $300 3) $150 – $200
Plate 296	1) $2,500 – $4,000 2) $300 – $400	Plate 307	1) $150 – $175 2) $275 – $375

			Plate 319	1)	$225 – $275 (without flower frog)
				2)	$175 – $275
				3)	$225 – $300

3) $150 – $200
4) $175 – $225
5) $225 – $300
6) $350 – $425

Plate 308 $400 – $475

Plate 309
1) $100 – $160
2) $175 – $275
3) $250 – $300
4) $100 – $150
5) $75 – $125
6) $100 – $150

Plate 310
1) $250 – $325
2) $225 – $290
3) $250 – $325
4) $175 – $225
5) $100 – $175 (with flower frog)
6) $200 – $275

Plate 311
1) $350 – $425
2) $375 – $450

Plate 312
1) $175 – $240
2) $275 – $375
3) $300 – $380 (with flower frog)
4) $175– $240

Plate 313 $425 – $525

Plate 314
1) $275 – $350 (without flower frog)
2) $450 – $500 (without flower frog)
3) $50 – $90
4) $60 – $100

Plate 315
1) $250 – $340
2) $325 – $425
3) $200 – $275

Plate 316
1) $200 – $275 (without flower frog)
2) $350 – $450 (without flower frog)

Plate 317
1) $200 – $250 (with lid)
2) $200 – $300
3) $75 – $140
4) $250 – $325

Plate 318
1) $225 – $300
2) $775 – $900
3) $250 – $325
4) $375 – $425
5) $200 – $275
6) $100 – $160

Plate 319
1) $225 – $275 (without flower frog)
2) $175 – $275
3) $225 – $300

Plate 320
1) $300 – $375
2) $325 – $400
3) $175 – $225
4) $225 – $300
5) $225 – $275
6) $250 – $300

Plate 321
1) $125 – $160
2) $125 – $190
3) $125 – $190

Plate 322
1) $250 – $325
2) $225 – $300
3) $225 – $290

Plate 323
1) $175 – $240 (pair)
2) $350 – $425
3) $175 – $240
4) $125 – $175
5) $325 – $400
6) $75 – $140

Plate 324
1) $75 – $140
2) $75 – $125
3) $75 – $125
4) $140 – $190
5) $75 – $140
6) $75 – $140

Plate 325
1) $75 – $100
2) $75 – $100
3) $125 – $200

Plate 326
1) $100 – $175
2) $200 – $275
3) $175 – $275

Plate 327
1) $275 – $375 (pair)
2) $200 – $300 (pair)

Plate 328
1) $300 – $375 (pair)
2) $150 – $250 (pair)

Plate 329
1) $250 – $325 (pair)
2) $225 – $300 (pair)
3) $200 – $250
4) $150 – $200
5) $200 – $250

Plate 330	1) $50 – $75		Plate 342	1) $125 – $175 (single)
	2) $75 – $110			2) $125 – $175 (single)
	3) $65 – $100			3) $100 – $175
	4) $75 – $140			4) $75 – $110
				5) $125 – $175
Plate 331	$100 – $150			6) $100 – $150
Plate 332	1) $50 – $85		Plate 343	1) $125 – $175 (single)
	2) $50 – $85			2) $140 – $185
	3) $45 – $65			3) $60 – $100
	4) $45 – $65			4) $150 – $250
	5) $100 – $140			5) $475 – $525
Plate 333	1) $225 – $300		Plate 344	1) $150 – $225
	2) $75 – $125			2) $150 – $225
	3) $325 – $400			3) $150 – $225
	4) $25 – $65			4) $75 – $140
	6) $550 – $650 (cup and saucer)			5) $85 – $150
	7) $50 – $75			6) $125 – $180
Plate 334	1) $45 – $80		Plate 345	1) $75 – $135
	2) $150 – $200			2) $75 – $145
	3) $75 – $140			3) $125 – $175
				4) $75 – $140
Plate 335	1) $85 – $150 (pair)			5) $50 – $85
	2) $50 – $90 (pair)			
	3) $50 – $75		Plate 346	1) $50 – $85
	4) $35 – $65			2) $75 – $120
	5) $50 – $85			3) $35 – $60
				4) $120 – $170
Plate 336	1) $150 – $200			5) $30 – $60
	2) $150 – $225			6) $75 – $135
	3) $75 – $150			
			Plate 347	1) $75 – $135
Plate 337	1) $175 – $225 (lid missing)			2) $75 – $135
	2) $30 – $60			3) $75 – $135
				4) $50 – $80
Plate 338	1) $150 – $225			5) $75 – $135
	2) $75 – $125			6) $75 – $135
	3) $75 – $125			
			Plate 348	1) $50 – $75
Plate 339	1) $275 – $375			2) $85 – $145
	2) $275 – $375			3) $30 – $60
				4) $40 – $75
Plate 340	1) $350 – $400			5) $40 – $75
	2) $275 – $325			6) $75 – $120
				7) $30 – $50 (sugar)
Plate 341	1) $175 – $140 (pair)			8) $30 – $50 (creamer)
	2) $125 – $175			
	3) $175 – $200		Plate 349	1) $50 – $85
	4) $150 – $200			2) $30 – $50
	5) $100 – $165			3) $45 – $80
	6) $200 – $275			4) $45 – $75
				5) $50 – $80

Plate 350	1) $30 – $55	Plate 360	$25 – $35
	2) $40 – $70		
	3) $40 – $70	Plate 361	$35 – $55
	4) $45 – $70		
	5) $50 – $80 (pair)	Plate 362	1) $25 – $30
			2) $25 – $35
Plate 351	$50 – $90		3) $25 – $30
Plate 352	1) $60 – $100	Plate 363	1) $200 – $275
	2) $35 – $65		2) $60 – $85
	3) $55 – $80		3) $200 – $275
	4) $40 – $60		4) $45 – $65
	5) $30 – $55		5) $30 – $35
	6) $40 – $60		6) $30 – $50
Plate 353	1) $100 – $150	Plate 364	1) $60 – $80
	2) $60 – $100		2) $20 – $35
	3) $55 – $85		3) $35 – $60
	4) $45 – $60 (creamer)		4) $30 – $50
	5) $55 – $70 (sugar)		5) $40 – $60
	6) $25 – $55		
		Plate 365	1) $225 – $300
Plate 354	1) $45 – $65		2) $200 – $275
	2) $40 – $60		
	3) $50 – $65	Plate 366	1) $175 – $225
	4) $25 – $40 (sugar)		2) $300 – $375
	5) $35 – $55		3) $150 – $200
	6) $25 – $35 (creamer)		
		Plate 367	1) $200 – $275
Plate 355	1) $135 – $170		2) $200 – $300
	2) $75 – $135		
	3) $55 – $85	Plate 368	1) $45 – $70
			2) $140 – $190
Plate 356	1) $55 – $85		3) $60 – $120
	2) $75 – $135		
	3) $55 – $90	Plate 369	1) $85 – $170
	4) $45 – $70		2) $85 – $170
	5) $35 – $65		
	6) $50 – $80	Plate 370	1) $125 – $175
	7) $25 – $55		2) $125 – $175
			3) $125 – $175
Plate 357	1) $50 – $80		
	2) $60 – $100 (pair)	Plate 371	1) $60 – $85
	3) $50 – $85		2) $65 – $95
	4) $30 – $55		3) $60 – $85
	5) $35 – $65 (with flower frog)		4) $25 – $35
			5) $30 – $50
Plate 358	$475 – $525		6) $30 – $50
Plate 359	1) $75 – $135	Plate 372	1) $350 – $450
	2) $55 – $80		2) $250 – $350
	3) $75 – $100		
	4) $65 – $100		

Plate 373	1) $25 – $40	Plate 379	1) $40 – $70 (pair)
	2) $40 – $60		2) $35 – $50 (kittens, each)
	3) $25 – $35		3) $30 – $50 (pair)
	4) $20 – $35		4) $35 – $60 (pair)
	5) $50 – $75		5) $30 – $55
	6) $45 – $80		6) $30 – $65
Plate 374	1) $80 – $135	Plate 380	1) $45 – $70
	2) $45 – $70		2) $45 – $60
			3) $60 – $85
Plate 375	1) $30 – $55		4) $55 – $80
	2) $35 – $65		5) $55 – $80
	3) $30 – $55		6) $40 – $70
	4) $25 – $35		
	5) $30 – $40	Plate 381	1) $55 – $80
	6) $30 – $45		2) $55 – $80
			3) $35 – $45
Plate 376	1) $45 – $70		
	2) $45 – $70	Plate 382	$175 – $250 (complete pamphlet)
	3) $65 – $125		
		Plate 399	$35 – $60 (complete pamphlet)
Plate 377	1) $45 – $65		
	2) $45 – $60	Plate 404	$50 – $80 (advertising card)
	3) $20 – $25		
	4) $20 – $25	Plate 406	$125 – $160 (postcard)
	5) $40 – $70		
		Plate 407	$10 – $25 (postcard)
Plate 378	1) $35 – $65		
	2) $65 – $100		
	3) $85 – $135		

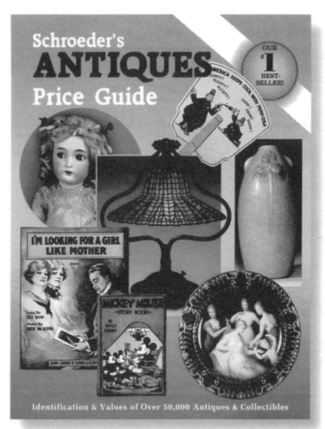